D1591347

Russian Armour 1941-1943

Russian Armour 1941-1943

by

Eric Grove

with illustrations by

The County Studios

Almark Publishing Co Ltd London

First Published 1977.

ISBN 0 85524 269 8

Distributed in the U. S. A. by
Squadron/Signal Publications Inc.,
3515E, Ten Mile Road,
Warren, Michigan 48091.

Printed in Great Britain by
Edwin Snell Printers,
Park Road, Yeovil,
Somerset,
for the publishers, Almark Publishing Co. Ltd.
49 Malden Way, New Malden,
Surrey KT3 6EA, England.

Contents

Acknowledgements

All pictures with the exception of those listed below are from the Imperial War Museum collection. Pages 6, 20, 23, 41, 45, 52, 59, 62, 65, Novosti.

The Shock

In the early hours of June 22nd 1941 the Germans struck the Soviet Union with over 3,300 tanks in 17 Panzer Divisions. There had been considerable warning, but Stalin prevented almost any countermeasures being taken until too late. The Soviet forces hit on the first day were in three (Special) Military Districts so designated because of their supposed ability to become 'Fronts' and to carry out immediate operations with existing forces. These Districts were composed of a number of armies each of which in turn normally deployed a mechanised corps as second echelon to deal with enemy breakthroughs.

In Colonel General F. I. Kuznetsov's Baltic (Special) Military District, which ran along the border with East Prussia the 8th Army had XII Mechanised Corps and the 11th Army III. XII Mechanised had 651 tanks out of its establishment of 1,031 and III had about 500. Only 105 of these 1,150 or so tanks were new models (almost all KVs) and of the total available vehicles the proportions out of service under repair were 16% and 45% respectively.

Further south the Western (Special) Military District held the vulnerable salient that jutted out to the Bug and followed the river south to Brest Litovsk. It was commanded by Colonel General Pavlov, whose supposed armoured expertise it was hoped would be of use in the case of a German attack. He deployed three armies, 3rd with XI Mechanised Corps around Vilno, 10th with VI Mechanised Corps around Bialystok and 4th with XIV Mechanised Corps around Brest. Pavlov held a further Mechanised Corps, XIII, in central reserve. Despite their crucial position these mechanised corps were a mixed bunch in terms of equipment. Major General M. G. Khatskilevich's VI was best off with perhaps 1,000 tanks and a small proportion of modern armour. One of its constituent divisions, 4th Tank, had 355 tanks of which 21 were T-34s and 10 KVs. XIV Mechanised Corps should have had an establishment of 1,025 tanks; 420 T-34s and 126 KVs. Actually Major General S. I. Oborin only had 508 obsolescent T-26 light tanks culled from the erstwhile NPP battalions. Akhlyustin's XIII Mechanised Corps was similarly equipped and Mostovenko's XI Mechanised had only 290 tanks of which a mere 24 were T-34s and 3 KVs.

Defending the northern approach to the Ukraine and the shortest German route to the vital areas in the industrial south was Colonel General N. P. Kirponos's Kiev (Special) Military District. Facing the Germans was 5th Army around Kovel with XXII Mechanised Corps and 6th Army around Lwow with IV Mechanised Corps. The VIII Mechanised Corps supported 26th Army deployed along the Hungarian border and Kirponos had three more mechanised corps in immediate reserve behind 5th and 6th Armies, Major General Karpezo's XV Feklenko's XIX and Rokosovskii's IX. None of these formations was near

Far left: Soviet tank riders scan the sky as they advance to the west of Kiev in the winter of 1943. The tanks are T-34/76Es. The tank riders are sitting on the rear decking where they can enjoy the engine warmth.

A German grenadier dug in by a Komsomolets tractor. The tractor could be used as a troop carrier or for towing artillery. It was armed with one DT machine gun. The practice of digging in by wrecked armoured vehicles was common in the German army since this afforded some degree of overhead protection.

its establishment, although VIII Mechanised Corps has 170 T-34s and KVs out of about 600 available machines. The XV had almost as many new mediums and heavies, 133 – but lacked artillery and trucks for its motorised infantry. XXII Mechanised Corps had some new armour in one of its tank divisions. These formations could each put both their divisions into the field but IX and XIX Mechanised Corps had only a single tank division ready for operational use, the 35th and 43rd respectively.

The mechanised corps stretched back for distances that ranged from 250km in the central sector to 400km in Kirponos' district. Communications were, therefore vital if the required counter attacks were to be concerted but the shortage of radios made this difficult. Often the only recourse was the civilian telephone system, which the Luftwaffe comprehensively destroyed in the opening hours. Bombers covered the roads and made the task of assembling the armoured forces difficult in the extreme. In such conditions it was perhaps surprising that any Soviet responses were made at all.

In Lithuania Kuznetsov immediately tried to combine his two Mechanised Corps for a counter attack under 8th Army Command against the flanks of the fast advancing Panzergruppe 4 which the Soviet commander assumed to be concentrated along the Telsit-Shauliya road. III Mechanised Corps would concentrate south of Rasienai and strike northwards towards XII Mechanised coming down from Shauliya. The former formation had already lost one of its tank divisions, the 5th, tied down trying to hold the river Niemen line against Hoth's Panzergruppe 3. The Division's tanks, T-26s and BTs, proved surprisingly difficult for the Germans to destroy but heavy attacks by the Luftwaffe depleted their strength and prevented the Russian attacks from being properly coordinated. The anti-tank gun and tank crews of 7th Panzer Division were able to outmanoeuvre and outshoot the disorganised Russians.

If the Germans were surprised by the strength of 5th Tank Division's resistance on the Niemen they were to be even more shocked when they met Kuznetsov's main counter attack at Rasienai, even though the strength of the counter attack was dissipated by faulty Russian tactics. 'To avoid the attentions of enemy aircraft' the Front Commander ordered his tanks to move in 'small columns'. This provided little protection from the Luftwaffe but did split up the Soviet vehicles into small groups of only limited effectiveness. German bombers and lack of fuel delayed the assembly of Shestopalov's XII Mechanised but the remaining tank division of III Mechanised Corps, 2nd, succeeded in catching 6th Panzer Division on the march. III Mechanised as a whole only had two KVs but the Germans were taken by surprise and the Soviet war diary reported the destruction of a German motorised regiment, 40 tanks and 40 guns. Unfortunately 2nd Tank Division now also stalled for lack of fuel.

The 1st Panzer Division now moved to rescue the 6th but was caught by the 84 tanks of Chernyakovskii's 28th Tank Division from XII Mechanised Corps. There were rather more KVs this time whose 75-110mm armour proved impervious to German fire. The PzKpfw III of 1st Panzer could do little against them except at close range from the flank with special PzGr 40 APCR shot. Normal high velocity rounds just bounced off or stuck in the armour; one KV-2 took over 70 hits. Only field and medium artillery and 88mm anti-aircraft guns could be sure of a kill, although smaller calibre fire might be able to break up a tank's tracks or shoot holes in the KV-2's wide gun barrel. Sometimes hand placed charges were the only answer.

Eventually, however, superior tactics told. The Germans were fighting in concentrated manoeuvrable masses under tight radio control, the Russians in small disorganised groups from which the older tanks could be shot away. The modern heavies were thus eventually isolated and neutralised. Soviet shooting was erratic. By the end of the 25th, 28th Tank had lost all its vehicles. The following day the two remaining tank divisions made one last effort but the Soviet tanks, unsupported by their own artillery, were shot up by the Germans' heavy guns emplaced in commanding positions. Taking advantage of the confusion 1st and 6th Panzer joined up. The Soviet survivors managed to escape being cut off and retreated, short of fuel and ammunition, into the marshy countryside. The Soviets had lost 180 tanks, including 29 KVs. The Germans had received a nasty shock but even as the tank battle had been raging Manstein's LVI Panzer Corps was outflanking it to the south against

A BT-7/2, a later mark of BT-7 which had a welded 'conical' turret. In this photograph the armour thicknesses have been painted on the tank. The BT-7 was armed with one 45 mm gun and a co-axial 7.62 mm DT machine gun. It weighed 13.8 tonnes.

little resistance. By the end of the day he had a bridgehead over the Dvina at Daugavpils. This, and the successes of Panzergruppe 3 to the south meant that North Western Front had been decisively outflanked.

In the centre the hapless Pavlov was struck by two infantry armies, outflanked by two Panzergruppen and steadily lost control. Communications were immediately cut and Lieutenant General Boldin, Pavlov's deputy, had to be sent to restore contact with Major General Golubev's 10th Army. Golubev had the powerful VI Mechanised Corps but little idea of how to use it, splitting the tanks away from their supporting motorised infantry. Of the tanks themselves about 30% were unserviceable, and some of the rest were immobile due to the Luftwaffe's efficient destruction of the Soviet fuel depots. As Pavlov issued orders which only showed his lack of comprehension of the situation Boldin got Khatskilevich to set about reassembling his Corps which once concentrated in the woods north east of Bialystok would strike northwards towards Grodno.

In the Grodno area itself 3rd Army's commander, cut off from all communication, had already ordered Mostovenko's small XI Mechanised into action. The three divisions of the Corps were spread over a wide area with the two tank divisions, 29th and 33rd, separated by 30 kilometres from each other and the Corps H.Q., with the motor rifle division a further 30 kilometres away still. These disconnected formations could do little to coordinate their actions for after only half an hour's preparation they were sent into action. Some tanks achieved an advance of 17 kilometres but the German anti-tank guns were able to cope with the attack. Soviet success was short lived and Grodno fell on the 23rd. VI Mechanised, which Khatskilevich had managed to re-assemble, advanced into the area under heavy Stuka attack, which adversely affected the morale of the Soviet tank crews. Fuel and communications were constantly in short supply; even the awesome T-34 was useless if it could neither move nor fight. Requests for fuel to be dropped by air went unheeded. Having advanced into the open these immobile and defenceless divisions were taken in flank by Hoth's tanks which split the regiments up into ill-controlled, outmanoeuvred companies which were destroyed in detail. The remains of 4th Tank Division fought a last stand west of Minsk. By June 29th the Corps had virtually ceased to exist. Its commander was dead and the cut off survivors tried to escape on foot.

To the south the 4th Army was ordered to attack towards Brest Litovsk with its XIV Mechanised Corps, supported if possible by XIII Mechanised. On the 23rd XIV got itself together and mounted its attack alone on a 20 kilometre front only to be quickly halted by the Germans' 37mm and 50mm anti-tank guns which had little trouble in penetrating the 16-25mm armour of the old Russian tanks. The attack was ill coordinated and there was no artillery preparation which might have cleared a way for the T-26s. Guderian's Panzergruppe was pressing on fast into the Soviet rear areas aiming at Minsk where the first great encirclement would be consummated. The only opposition came from isolated groups of tanks manned by bewildered crews which could soon be put out of action by the German PzKpfw III and IV. The Russians now tried to concentrate forces to stop the dangerous enemy advance and to break out of potential encirclement. Available tanks and infantry were put into an attack on Slonim on the 25th but the well controlled German fire from 50mm and 75mm guns again had little trouble in penetrating the lightly armoured Soviet vehicles and the attack was driven off. A new, but badly equipped mechanised corps, XX with but few tanks was flung into the breach but it soon lost all armour and was reduced to fighting as an infantry formation.

On the 27th the advanced units of Panzergruppen 2 and 3 joined at Minsk. As those surviving tanks in the 'pocket' were destroyed in their desperate, isolated attempts to break out, the German armoured spearheads kept going towards the Berezina and Smolensk. On the 29th, Pavlov, a broken man, was dismissed and returned to Moscow to face trial and the execution squad. He was replaced by Yeremenko who had been transferred from the Far East. As Western Front's tank strength was reduced to about 145 vehicles, more armour was desperately needed to halt the German drive. Already on the 25th Marshal Budenny's 'Reserve Army Group' had been formed roughly along the line of the old Soviet border, with a second echelon around Smolensk itself. One of the formations assigned was Major General Vinogradov's VII Mechanised Corps, a well equipped formation with 1,000 tanks including significant quantities of T-34s and KVs. Originally assigned to Stavka (i.e. Central High Command) reserve on the 24th the Corps was continuously diverted to new destinations until on the 26th its staff and tanks arrived at Smolensk by rail. Here it was given operational dispositions as part of 20th Army, one of Budenny's front line formations. Unfortunately the tendency to disperse Mechanised Corps was still prevalent. Remizov, the Army Commander, sent Colonel I. G. Kreizer's crack 1st Moscow Motor Rifle Division to Orsha on the main Minsk-Smolensk motor road and the rest of the Corps was strung out to the north in a defensive line.

On the 2nd July Panzergruppe 2, in the shape of 18th Panzer Division, got a bridgehead over the Berezina at Borisov against stiff opposition from the tanks and men of the local Armoured Forces Training College. Other crossings were soon obtained down to Bobruisk. Yeremenko, who took over control of Reserve Army Group on July 1st, saw 1st Moscow Motor Rifle Division as a suitable weapon against the German breakthrough and the formation moved up from Orsha with its T-26s, BTs, T-34s and KV-2s. On the 3rd German air reconnaissance reported the advance of "Strong enemy armoured columns with at least 100 heavy tanks advancing along both sides of the Borisov-Smolensk road in the area of Orsha. Among them very heavy, hitherto unobserved models" (the massive KV2s). The two armoured forces met six miles east of Borisov near Lipki village. The new Soviet tanks made a great impression but their effect was decisively dissipated by deploying them in ones and twos among small groups of older tanks.

The Soviet division was pressed back upon the Dniepr but despite losses to German air attack continued to keep up the pressure on the Germans, even if the tactics remained tragically simple. On July 5th near Tolochino an unsupported line of ten T-26s attacked a single 50mm anti-tank gun of 18th Panzer's 101st Motorised Rifle Regiment: only one

A German artilleryman passes a knocked out KV2. Though very heavily armoured by contemporary standards the KV2 was slow and unstable. The 152 mm howitzer required an extra loader to handle the bulky ammunition.

managed to escape. Unsophisticated dispersed Soviet tactics continued to be the Achilles heel of the modern tanks too. Once the first terror had worn off even the German infantry soon found ways of defeating them.

On July 7th more Soviet tanks hit 101st Motorised Regiment. A 152mm shell from one KV-2 demolished the 50mm gun which had proved so effective against the T-26s and the Soviet tank rolled through the rest of the German anti-tank line. Soon, however, the clumsy vehicle got stuck, but this did not stop it from continuing to send its 152mm shells into the German positions. Carrying grenades strapped together to form explosive charges German infantrymen rushed the monster. Two charges were thrown and the KV's turret mechanism was jammed by the blast. Now the Germans climbed onto the tank and a 2nd Lieutenant pushed a single grenade down the gaping 152mm barrel. It exploded a shell in the gun and the turret hatch was opened as the survivors of the shambles inside tried to get out. Before they could, another set of grenades was thrown through the hatch. The KV's ammunition exploded and the massive turret was blown into a nearby field.

As early as July 2nd the seriousness of the situation had led to Timoshenko himself being placed in command of the vital Western Front. The Marshal was disturbed at Panzergruppe 3's penetration towards the upper Dvina at Vitebsk and prepared to strike at its southern flank with the remaining divisions of VII Mechanised – about 400 tanks – and the newly arrived V Mechanised Corps. The latter had been redeployed with its 300 tanks from the Far East as a precautionary measure in May. With the rest of 16th Army it was originally intended for Kirponos in the south west but on the 26th June it was ordered to the Smolensk area. Now the Corps, still without its infantry, was to strike north from Orsha with VII Mechanised towards Senno in a 'decisive offensive'. It was planned to advance some 100 km and even the Soviet Command was disturbed about such an exposed use of mechanised forces with no support from the air or other ground forces.

On the 6th the attack began. Despite little protection from the air, and a tendency to use their tanks in the usual piecemeal groups, the two Corps managed to advance on Senno but then they ran into the northern spearheads of Panzergruppe 2. By the 8th a major series of tank battles was in progress. These Soviet crews were seasoned veterans who handled their tanks with some skill. At the first clash the advancing Germans ran into a well laid and camouflaged tank ambush. The Soviet tanks attacked the German flanks and tried to take the enemy in the rear. The Germans still retained a tactical edge but this was countered by the T-34's robustness and heavy firepower. One shrugged off the attentions of four PzKpfw III and then, despite being hit several times, drove straight over a 37mm anti-tank gun which was earning the rueful nickname of 'the German Army's door knocker'. This particular tank motored on for nine miles deep into the German rear until, despite its wide tracks, it got stuck in marshy ground and was finished off by a 100mm heavy gun.

Back at the front German Stukas threw their weight into the scales which were slowly tipping against the Russians. The few available Soviet 37mm anti-aircraft guns were proving insufficient. Nevertheless the Soviet 76.2mm tank guns, when fired accurately, were proving their capacity to deal with any German vehicle and even the older Soviet tanks knocked out their share of German vehicles. The battle raged on through the day and night but ammunition and fuel shortages began to tell. The Soviets began to leave the littered battlefield to the Germans. Timoshenko's last readily available mechanised force had been destroyed and the German tanks continued to drive on to Smolensk, which fell on July 16th.

On Kirponos' South West Front 5th and 6th Armies quickly sent in the available units of their Mechanised Corps to reinforce the defensive infantry screen. Kirponos, however, planned to mass his Mechanised Corps for a counter attack bringing the VIII up from the south and joining it with his three northern reserve corps, IX, XV and XIX as well as IV and XXII. He wished to strike into the flanks of the advancing Germans west of Dubno and Lutsk. Some units had to cover over 300 kilometres to their assembly points. Nevertheless the southern formations were relatively well equipped, not only with T-34s and KVs but numbers of T-28 mediums to stiffen the ranks of the BTs and T-26s. The T-28s were good tanks although their high sides made them rather vulnerable and their crews could not cover their immediate vicinity against 'stalkers'. IV Mechanised had some T-35 heavies. Kirponos also deployed a few experimental heavy self propelled guns, the SU-14 with a 152mm gun-howitzer mounted in the rear of the T-35 chassis and the SU-100Y with the powerful 130mm gun on the T-100/SMK chassis (SU-*Samokhodnaya Ustanovka*-Self Propelled Mount).

The strain of moving the impractical T-35s over long distances proved too much. The Germans did not report engaging any in action. All those encountered had been abandoned, either broken down or out of fuel. They were dismissed as mere '*Kinderschrecke*' – things to frighten children. The T-34s proved rather more impressive. One of the first examples encountered in the south stood up to no less than twenty-three 37mm hits without damage. Only the 24th round aimed at the turret ring jammed the turret and forced the Soviet tank to withdraw.

As major incursions were made into Kirponos' right the Soviets were forced to respond without proper preparation. XV and VIII Mechanised Corps were ordered to strike from the south, but the former was stuck in difficult boggy roadless terrain west of Brody and the latter was still redeploying from Uman. Only 10th Tank Division from XV Mechanised was able to go into action near Radekhov and a major tank battle developed

A Russian officer observes from a BT-7 (V). This tank is recognisable as a commander's model by its frame antenna around the turret.

A T-26B-1 (V) commanders tank with frame antenna precedes an OT-130 flame throwing version of the T-26. The T-26B-1 (V) had a 45 mm gun while the OT-130 had a machine gun mounted co-axially with its main armament.

with the 15th Panzer Regiment, 11th Panzer Division. The scattered Russians operated as usual in small groups and were eventually outmanoeuvred and defeated, although it took a whole morning to destroy 20 tanks. The battle was rejoined the next day. XV Mechanised's 37th Tank Division after extricating itself had been sent on a wild goose chase against mythical German tanks but now met the real thing. 36th Panzer Regiment of 14th Panzer Division claimed nine T-28s in a mid morning engagement and before the day was out there were more tank versus tank clashes in which Soviet tactical inadequacies led to 149 more tanks being lost. Further south where the Germans were breaking through toward Lwow, 6th Army sent IV Mechanised into action but German *Panzerjägers* were able to hold off the badly handled Russian tanks. One tank division was uselessly wasted when its commander led it straight into a swamp.

On June 25th Kirponos ordered his main counter attack, a powerful armoured blow against both flanks of the developing 'panzer corridor'. VIII and XIV Mechanised Corps were combined as a 'Front Mobile Group' and would strike upwards from Brody to Berestechko (VIII) and from Toropuv to Radekhov (XV). The IX and XIX Mechanised Corps would be placed under the command of Potapov's 5th Army and after concentrating in the cover of the woods north of Rovno would attack south towards Dubno and Brody. The attack was planned for 09.00 on the 26th and the Russians struggled to get their forces into some kind of shape. The battered XV Mechanised could again only get one division into the field and was reinforced by the 8th Tank Division from Vlasov's unfortunate IV Mechanised Corps. The powerful VIII Mechanised was still incomplete with less than half its tanks available for action; 34th Tank Division had 150 and 12th Tank Division only 60. The terrain was very difficult with much marsh and swamp and numerous river lines a severe trial of the skill and initiative of the under trained Soviet tank crews and staff officers, and to show up the lack of proper support services. The Russians were facing five well coordinated panzer divisions with almost 800 tanks manned by well trained crews at the height of their powers.

Where the Russian tanks met German armour they tended to be held but at the bridgeheads over the Styr held by the German 57th Infantry Division, the T-34s and KVs of VIII Mechanised Corps were able to make some progress, brushing aside the fire of 37mm anti-tank guns. Some tanks penetrated quite deeply into the German positions before being dealt with by artillery at point blank range. At Berestechko the Germans rushed up 47mm self-propelled tank destroyers and 88mm anti-aircraft guns to keep back the Russian tanks which had crashed into 16th Panzer's Infantry Brigade. Attacks by the Luftwaffe created confusion amongst Soviet units coming up from the south and set Russian tanks and trucks alight but still the Germans were significantly slowed down. By the end of the day Panzergruppe I's war diary reported that almost all units were engaged in 'heavy fighting'.

During the night Kirponos swung his southerly attackers round to the right with Ryabyshev's VIII Mechanised to advance on Dubno and XV against the Berestechko bridgehead from the west. Hard pressed from the air Ryabyshev was still having problems concentrating his forces and formed a 'Mobile Group' from 34th Tank Division, another tank regiment and a motor cycle regiment under the unlikely command of a political officer, Brigade Commissar N. K. Popiel. On the 26th this was now launched into the rear of XLVIII Panzer Corps. Popiel had some success against 16th Panzer Division's support columns but the Soviet attacks remained disorganised and consequently suffered grievously. XLVIII Panzer claimed no less than 62 tanks destroyed and III Panzer Corps 30 in heavy fighting with IX Mechanised Corps. German air reconnaissance reported the position of Popiel's Mobile Group in the woods west of Dubno early on the morning of the 28th and 16th Panzer Division swung to meet it. By the end of the day this formation was claiming the destruction of a total of 83 light and medium Soviet tanks and three KVs since the 26th.

On June 29th the pressure was kept up, although some Soviet tanks were able to penetrate Dubno from the west and the Russians put in what the Germans called 'violent tank supported attacks' from the west near Rovno. The 16th Panzer Division, reinforced by infantry, were able to keep the Soviet formations apart. By the end of the day Popiel's force was surrounded but on the 29th Potapov was ordered to mount another counter attack with both XXII and IX Mechanised Corps out of the wooded country near Klevany. III Panzer Corps was hard pressed and although the Germans hit back heavily with air attacks the German's Corps' advance was halted.

During the warm night of the 29th-30th Popiel tried to break out toward the south. Desperate close in fighting saw Soviet tanks attempting to ram their German counterparts. Kirponos ordered one last desperate attack: it failed. Twenty more tanks of the encircled group were destroyed in yet another break out attempt, and then German tanks went into action to complete the destruction of the cut-off armour. By July 1st the Germans reported only isolated Russian tanks and scattered units remaining south of Dubno. Popiel's group had ceased to exist as a fighting force and the survivors, like so many Soviet troups in those terrible summer days, tried to make it back to friendly territory on foot.

Kirponos' counter attacks had had some success but their cost was enormous. By the first of July 16th Panzer Division alone was claiming 261 Soviet tanks destroyed in the fighting around Dubno. The lack of spares and repair facilities meant that even minor mechanical ailments led to a tank's destruction by its own crew: 58 of the 119 tanks lost by XXII Mechanised Corps had to be given up in this way. The lack of control of commanders, like Potapov who had failed to coordinate the northerly mechanised corps with each other and the 'Front Mobile Group', had allowed the Germans to quickly take advantage of Soviet dispersion and deploy local superiority to wear down Russian strength. Nevertheless casualties had been heavy on both sides, and by the beginning of July a new Soviet line of defence was starting to form. Rundstedt's Army Group South had not yet succeeded in decisively outflanking South Western Front. Given what was happening in the north this was something of a success.

Up in Latvia Manstein had succeeded in

unhinging the Soviet defence. A third army, 27th, had been forming in Baltic (Special) Military District on the outbreak of war. It was located around the Dvina which LVI Panzer Corps had just swept across and now Stavka released XXI Mechanised Corps to give it some armoured bite. The teeth were not very sharp, General D. D. Lelyushenko only had 98 old tanks, some BT-7s, just transferred from training duties. But they were better than nothing, especially as the officers were of high quality. 46th Tank Division's attack, under Kuptsov who had distinguished himself in the Far East, penetrated to the streets of Dvinsk on the 28th. Again the Russians used ramming tactics. German air attacks prevented reinforcements arriving and the Russian tanks soon began to run out of fuel and ammunition. However eventually the 42nd Tank Division was brought into action along the Dvina. Manstein described the situation as 'quite critical' as he suffered heavy casualties, but German reinforcements moved in and Lelyushenko was soon reduced to only 7 tanks and forced back. The survivors of the XII Mechanised, the honourable losers at Rasienai, were now prepared for a new blow against Manstein. They could muster only 35 tanks in all, commanded by the Front Chief of Armoured Forces Administration, Colonel P. P. Poluboyarov. Outnumbered and outmanoeuvred, they stood little chance of doing more than slowing Manstein down, although the distinguished German commander did complain in his memoirs of 'resistance tougher and more methodical than in the first days of the campaign'.

Now the Soviet Command strove to build up a new defensive line along the old border. It needed tanks, and I Mechanised Corps was redeployed down from the Northern Flank, leaving only one Mechanised Corps, X (1st and 24th Tank Divisions) to support the defence of Leningrad from the north against the increasingly threatening Finns. By July 2nd I Mechanised Corps' 3rd Division was deployed and ready ten miles north east of Pskov. When 1st Panzer took the Velikaya crossing at Ostrov the tanks moved down to intercept. This division was well equipped with KV-1s and 2s. As before, the German 37mm anti-tank guns proved useless against their thick hulls and turrets. The Germans had to resort to 150mm field howitzers firing shells designed to penetrate concrete pill-boxes. Thirteen Soviet tanks fell to one such weapon, and their morale restored the German infantrymen set about dealing with the others with demolition charges. The Soviet attack was turned back. As the Germans advanced on Pskov 3rd Tank Division kept up some pressure with BTs but despite more desperate ramming tactics the well handled PzKpfw IIIs with their 50mm guns were more than adequate to deal with the Soviets with their maximum armour protection of only 22mm. Tanks built with speed as their major protection needed more skilled crews than the Red Army could provide in July 1941. Pskov fell on July 9th and the Russian forces, including I Mechanised, fell back to the Luga.

On July 1st the war spread south when the Rumanian/German right wing of Rundstedt's Army Group South began to move against the Soviet South Front, formed by General I. V. Tyulenev out of the old Odessa Military District. Tyulenev had three mechanised corps assembling behind his front lines, II, XVI and XVIII and the first of these, together with a rifle and cavalry corps, was pushed against German 11th Army's bridgeheads over the Prut north of Kishinev. As the *Panzerjägers* of the German infantry divisions held off the lightly protected Russian tanks, Tyulenev began to lose his armour to the north where the pressure on Kirponos continued. Here, German tanks, concentrating their strength on a narrow front, were finally able to break

The interior of the turret of a KV-1. The breach of the 76.2 mm gun is in the centre with the gunners position on the left and the radio operator/machine gunners position on the right. The magazines for the DT machine gun are visible on the top right and also to the lower right of the breach. Also visible are the eye pieces of the twin periscopes to the top left and right.

through and were only 15 km from Kiev by July 11th. Again the battered Mechanised Corps had to be thrown in against the German flanks. The Soviet armoured formations were now but shadows of their former selves, IX Mechanised Corps had only 64 tanks left, XXII less than 20. With the remnants of XIX Mechanised Corps these would form up under Potopov's command to strike south towards Berdichev and Lyubar. To the south the 6th Army was left with 8th Tank Division, returned to Vlasov's IV Mechanised Corps, the remains of XV Mechanised Corps organised into 'composite detachments' under the overall command of Major General S. D. Ogurtsov and the still deploying elements of XVI Mechanised from Southern Front. The latter's commander, Major General A. D. Sokolov, was placed in overall command of the available units of his own Corps and Ogurtsov's 'composite detachments', the whole being known as 'Operational Group Berdichev'. These forces now provided the armoured weight to the mixed groups of artillery supported tanks and infantry that thrust their way into the German flanks on July 9th and 10th. Stukas once more battered the unfortunate Russians and the Germans quickly moved up reinforcements to keep the persistent enemy at bay. The fighting went on on the southern flank for five days and on the northern for seven but the Germans were able

to keep out of trouble and continued to push their advanced armour forward on Kiev and into the deep rear of South Western Front. Apart from scratch forces, which included a single tank regiment thrown together with NVKD internal security troops, paratroopers and trainee artillerymen on the approaches to Kiev, Kirponos had little left to stop them. His front had finally and decisively been split into two.

By the end of July, 1941 the western territories of the U.S.S.R. were littered with the remains of the Soviet armoured forces; T-26s knocked out in desperate counter-attacks or left fuel-less lined up on White Russian roads; BTs blown over by German bombs or burned out after numerous anti-tank hits; T-28s surrounded by wreckage after their ammunition had exploded; T-35s driven off roads after their petrol or over-stressed mechanical parts had given out; perhaps most futile of all T-34s driven into bogs by inexperienced drivers and KV-1s and -2s penetrated by hastily brought up heavy artillery after isolated counter attacks. When the Soviet forces were trapped in the Minsk 'Pocket' on July 3rd the Germans put the number of knocked out or captured tanks at 2,282, about the number with which they had conquered France the previous year. On July 10th Panzergruppe 1 put its tally of Soviet tanks knocked out at 1,830. On the central and southern fronts alone, therefore, the first three weeks of fighting had seen the equivalent number of Soviet tanks destroyed that the Germans had fielded in the invasion on July 22nd. And the slaughter had only just begun.

Disaster and Hope

As Smolensk fell and the advanced German armoured spearheads reached out 80 kilometres further east to Yartsevo and Yalnaya, the Russians attempted desperately to strike back. Four armies each accompanied by a tank division were brought up from Reserve Front, to be combined with the survivors of the previous month's encirclement battles into five 'Army Groups'. As these were launched against the advanced German forces in fierce repeated counter-attacks the encircled 20th and 16th Armies, also kept up the pressure. Soviet tactics were primitive frontal assaults and only shortage of German ammunition prevented heavier Russian casualties in both men and weapons. The Germans were claiming fifty tanks knocked out per day. The two encircled Soviet Armies were eventually ordered to break out; 20th Army still had 65 operational tanks left and used them to batter a way out through to the German lines. When fighting ceased in the Smolensk 'Pocket' on the 5th August the Germans claimed 3,205 tanks captured or destroyed. In addition 200 Soviet tanks were lost in the Roslavl encirclement.

Far to the north in the Leningrad sector I Mechanised Corps carried out a Soviet attempt at encirclement. Manstein's Panzer Corps was becoming increasingly exposed in its advance on Novgorod as it attempted to struggle through the marshy forests south west of Lake Ilmen. Now as 8th Panzer Division passed Soltsi 3rd Tank Division struck down from the north and 21st Tank Division from the south east. The tanks were used to support some of 11th Army's six infantry divisions in an attempt to score a decisive success for Marshal Voroshilov the new High Commander of the entire north west 'axis'. Locals guided the armoured units through the swamps and the Russian attack had some success at first. 8th Panzer Division was cut in two and separated from its accompanying 3rd Motorised Division. Repeated attacks were beaten off after close range fighting in which heavy artillery was again used at point blank range to beat off the Russian tanks. Eventually the Germans brought up reinforcements and succeeding in reconnecting their formations once more. The Russians suffered again from lack of control and concentration but they had succeeded in inflicting another nasty shock on the over confident Germans which helped delay their assault over the River Luga.

Now all efforts were put into defending this river line but there was not much armour available to back it up. The Soviet tank divisions had already suffered serious casualties in trying to stop the German advance. The 21st for example was still engaged around Lake Ilmen, some of its broken down tanks being expended as dug-in pill boxes, while other more mobile machines mounted counter attacks against the German infantry of IX Corps advancing on Staraya Russa. Yet more casualties were suffered as 20mm anti-

Far left: A troop commander leads his T-34/76Bs. Visible on the turret side is the lozenge with the company or platoon number and callsign. The big turret hatch proved to be unsatisfactory in action since grenades could be thrown into the tank. The commander has a flag for signalling to the tanks unequipped with radios.

Soviet infantry move up in support of three KV-1s. Visible on the rear of the turret is the mounting for the DT machine gun. The broad tracks of the KV series allowed these tanks, like the T-34, to wade through mud and snow which stopped or delayed their German opponents.

aircraft guns found the weak spots of T-26s and BTs and demolition charges were used to good effect against isolated KVs. 1st Tank Division was brought down from the Finnish Front to provide the armoured centre of a 'High Command Reserve' force but it had also suffered severely. At the beginning of July, Finnish and German forces had gone over to the attack along Finland's long border with the U.S.S.R. West of Kandalaksha 1st Tank Division lost many tanks although Soviet resistance stopped the attacks of German XXXVI Corps aiming at the Murmansk railway.

Luckily for the Russians the Finns were more concerned with regaining their lost territories than helping the Germans capture Leningrad and their advance ground to a standstill at the beginning of September. While it lasted, however, it put an enormous strain on the Soviet defences, especially after the Germans opened their offensive west of Leningrad on 8th August; on the 13th North Front was calling for the immediate reinforcement by 250 tanks. None was immediately available as reserve armoured forces had been concentrated in XXI Mechanised Corps which was allocated to support a new 34th Army to counter attack below Lake Ilmen. After some progress it was encircled and destroyed. LVI Panzer Corps alone claimed the destruction or capture of 141 tanks. At the other end of the lake 21st Tank Division now allocated to another new Army, 48th, strove vainly to defend Novgorod and the main Moscow – Leningrad railway which the Germans cut at Chudovo. This division was steadily running out of tanks.

Luga itself had been passed by the main German advance further downstream but it continued to block the German supply lines. On the 13th August a major assault was mounted to outflank the town from the east. German infantry got across the river but were then struck by Soviet tanks from 1st Tank Division. Groups of T-28s and T-26s cornered groups of German infantry companies in the dense, marshy forests but were held off by 37mm anti-tank guns, demolition charges placed in front of tracks and grenades thrust through open hatches. The Russians still had problems in coordinating tanks and infantry so that the latter could effectively protect the former but nevertheless for a week they held the Germans in front of the River Oredezh.

Leningrad was still producing KVs for the entire Red Army and on August 26th Stalin allowed North Front to take four days' production for its own purposes. New KVs were driven by scratch crews straight from their factories to the front line. Some tanks were only partly painted and were manned by the workers who had made them, men and women. At the other end of the scale the small, practically useless T-27 tankettes were pressed back into combat use and thrown into the struggle. Tanks which had broken down and were incapable of further mobile use were employed as pill-boxes in the increasingly formidable city defences. Although the main German assault on Leningrad was planned for 8th September the German forces advancing on the southern axis via Novgorod began their attack on the 6th. German 50mm anti-tank and 88mm anti-aircraft guns kept 21st Tank Division at bay, still further depleting its stock of tanks. By the end of September it had run out completely. On September 8th Leningrad was cut off completely when Schusselburg fell.

Now the main German assault went in. Fighting was heavy and as the days wore on the Russians threw in their limited number of KVs as mobile reserves. But accurate shooting, quick thinking and good use of ground by German tanks could still overcome the Soviet tanks' thick armour and heavy armament. Limited Soviet counter attacks by untrained and nervous crews could only have a temporary effect as Zhukov, the new Leningrad commander, tried to get the city's defences into better shape. But the Germans had already decided to leave the city under siege. All efforts would now go into the capture of Moscow.

Far to the south the Russians were suffering their heaviest defeat yet. On August 21st Hitler had confirmed his intention to concentrate on the flanks, Leningrad and the south. Guderian's Panzergruppe 2, already making gains in this direction, was to strike southwards over the Desna into the right flank of South Western front. The Russians brought up more tanks to deal with this threat; Yeremenko's new Bryansk Front had only one tank division but Stalin offered more armour from Stavka reserve, two brigades with a few KVs and two or three tank battalions. Around Pochep the 108th and 110th Tank Brigades attacked 17th Panzer Division in the sector of South Western Front's northernmost Army, the 48th, but the German tanks' advance was not stopped and by the end of the first week in September they had made a decisive breakthrough. The Russians, thinking that the Germans had not changed their strategic emphasis, spread their effort over too wide a front. There had been in places some concentration of armoured resources but generally the tanks had been spread out in ones and twos among the infantry.

Coming up from the south were the spearheads of Kleist's Panzergruppe 1. This had already trapped 6th, 12th and part of 18th Armies, together with their armoured units, the survivors of the previous heavy fighting around Berdichev. Many Soviet troops were able to fight their way out eastwards to safety, but when the pocket finally gave up the Germans found another 317 destroyed or abandoned Soviet tanks littering the battlefield.

This meant that there was little or no armour to hold the Dniepr and the Germans swept across at Kremenchug. There was nothing the increasingly trapped South Western Front could do; 10th Tank Division was down to a miserable twenty operational tanks. Budenny new 'Axis' High Commander called for a complete withdrawal out of the Dniepr bend but Stalin, perhaps not yet fully aware of the enormity of the situation and still putting faith in Yeremenko's counter attacks, refused. Budenny was replaced by Timoshenko. On the 14th the German armoured spearheads linked up between Lokhvitsa and Lubny. The Russians tried to break out of the encirclement and Kirponos himself was killed in the attempt. Potopov was captured. The remnants of South West Front continued to batter against the eastern wall of the German ring. 9th Cavalry Division, with tank and air support, gave Guderian some anxious moments at Romny. Further north Yeremenko kept up the pressure with armour supported infantry attacks south of Novgorod Severskii. Nevertheless the German ring held and when pockets of resistance in the Dniepr bend were finally crushed the Germans claimed 824 tanks destroyed or captured and 665,000 prisoners in this the biggest of all battles of encirclement. The Smolensk pocket had netted less than half the number of men but almost four times as many tanks: such was the Red Army's tank shortage.

The Russians seemed beaten and the time had now come for the assault on Moscow – 'Operation Typhoon' which began on September 30th. To face the German assault forces which included three out of four Panzergruppen with 14 Panzer Divisions and 1700 tanks and assault guns the three Soviet Fronts, Western, Reserve and Bryansk could muster about 770 tanks. Most of these were from Colonel General Koniev's Western Front which had 483. Older Soviet models predominated, Koniev for example had only 45 T-34s and KVs. Most of this armour was deployed in 13 independent tank brigades and there was also one surviving tank division. The depleted Russian armoured forces were now decisively outnumbered to add to their problems of tactical inexperience and unsophistication.

At first, although counter attacks by KVs disrupted Guderian's preliminary attack to secure his southern flank, the Panzers seemed to have everything their own way once more. Yeremenko flung depleted tank brigades in isolated counter attacks against Guderian's advancing Panzergruppe 2. Reinforcements were rushed up, including Lelyushenko's I Guards Rifle Corps which contained 4th and 11th Tank Brigades, two of 22 such new formations which had just been assembled by Lelyushenko in his previous post as Deputy Commander of the Main Armoured Forces Administration. These formations were well equipped; 4th had a high proportion of T-34s among its 64 tanks as well as seven KVs. It had assembled at Prudboi, near Stalingrad and consisted of the instructors and cadets of the Kharkov tank training school as well as recently recovered tank crews wounded in earlier battles. The Brigade's commander was Colonel M. Katukov, who soon showed himself to be an armoured leader of above average skill.

On October 4th Katukov pressed home a counter attack with his first available tank battalion against 4th Panzer Division advancing towards Mtsensk. As more tanks arrived they were sent forward with infantry riding on the T-34s. The riflemen were used to 'fix' the German tanks while the Russian armour attacked from the flanks. Experienced Russian instructors and crews exploited their T-34s' ar-

mour and firepower, staying out of effective reach of the PzKpfw III and IV. In the latest version the Russian 76.2mm tank gun could penetrate well over 50mm of armour at 2,000 yards range and 70 at 500. It was not just sloping 45mm armour which protected the Russian crews, for the T-34s displayed a new found agility: good power to weight ratio and wide tracks were exploited to sweep over soft going far more easily than the narrow tracked German vehicles. When snow fell that evening and quickly melted, the T-34s were able to make their escape through the resulting mud.

On the 11th Katukov mounted another counter attack against the flanks of a chastened 4th Panzer Division, struggling to enter Mtsensk along the muddy and shell cratered road. The T-34s were able to sweep down and onto the exposed German flanks spread out over 25 kilometres south east of the town. Now it was the Russians who were able to concentrate tactical superiority, due to the superior mobility of their tanks. The Germans could not respond, for their tanks were stuck floundering in a muddy morass. Now it was the Germans who were destroyed in small and isolated groups. Casualties were heavy; between the 14th and 16th the Russians claimed 150 tanks knocked out from 3rd and 4th Panzer Divisions. Many would be repaired but the shock to German morale was considerable. As Guderian put it in his memoirs: "Up to now we had enjoyed tank superiority, but from now on the situation was reversed. The prospect of rapid decisive victories was fading in consequence". In November Katukov was promoted to Major General and the brigade was renamed 1st Guards Tank Brigade in honour of its success. It became the elite tank formation of the Soviet Army, later growing to a division and still later to a Corps. Katukov called his men the Army's 'Professors

A Komsomolets tractor tows a 37 mm anti-tank gun and limber while the crew hitch a ride. The scene is the winter of 1941 in the Kalinin region. The Komsomolets tractor was adapted as the chassis for some of the earliest tank destroyers to be deployed by the Soviet Union.

of Tank Warfare' and they set the standard as the Soviet armed forces dragged themselves out of the confusion of the opening months of combat.

Although 2nd Panzer Army had by now ground to a halt the Germans were still able to make gains in the north. An attempt to use the defenders in a more mobile role failed as the High Command insisted on a linear defence. There was little chance, therefore of concentrated flanking blows against German weak points, where the Soviet armour could have been used to best effect. The Germans succeeded in their planned encirclements and the Russians were ground to destruction. By mid-October the Germans were claiming more masses of prisoners and booty; 673,000 Red Army soldiers captured, 1,242 tanks captured or destroyed, the latter inflated by non-operational vehicles captured in depots or under repair. Another sacrifice of men and machines had been offered up to the seemingly invincible Wehrmacht.

Yet, despite their successes, the Germans were not feeling very invincible as their drive on Moscow was reduced to a crawl in the Autumn mud. And there were yet more Soviet formations available to bar their way. On October 6th six tank brigades and an equivalent number of infantry divisions were rushed to the line being built north and south of Mozhaisk to block the direct route to Moscow about 130 kilometres west of the city. They were eventually joined by ten more new tank brigades as formations from all over the Soviet Union, from the Urals, Central Asia and the Far East were rushed to the defence of the national capital. Forces were also redeployed from other sectors of the line, including Katukov's Tank Brigade, personally ordered by Stalin to reinforce the Mozhaisk Line on October 16th. Its commander insisted that it redeploy on its own tracks due to the danger of air attack if it moved by train. The brigade was soon in position having suffered no losses in its northward journey. On October 10th all available forces were put under the command of a new Western Front Commander, Zhukov.

Holding the vital central Mozhaisk axis itself, L. A. Govorov's 5th Army deployed the crack Siberian 32nd Rifle Division supported by the T-34s and KV-2s of 18th and 19th Tank Brigades on the ancient and hilly battlefield of Borodino. They were fiercely attacked by 10th Panzer Division and the S.S. Motorised Division, Das Reich, the Soviet armour being thrown against any potential enemy breakthrough. Where available, 88mm anti-aircraft guns provided defence from the new Russian tanks but, as usual, more desperate measures had to be adopted such as anti-tank mines wedged under the rear turrets of the T-34s. Eventually weight of German firepower told and the Russian positions were penetrated. On October 19th Mozhaisk fell but the German attack was now becoming very slow. By the end of the month Shelkovka and Dorokhovo was still being contested less than two kilometres further east. Two comparatively well equipped tank brigades supported a Mongolian motor rifle division in its attempt to recapture Shelkovka. The German and French infantry holding the position had few weapons to deal with the Soviet T-34s and were forced to retreat.

The right wing of Panzergruppe 4 was also slowly penetrating the Soviet Defensive Line to the south around Maloyaroslavets but it soon ran into more well equipped tank units. T-34s swept down from the surrounding hills to inflict heavy casualties. Eventually 88mm anti-aircraft guns succeeded in driving them off but the Soviet armour continued to be rather more than a nuisance. German tanks bogged down in the soft going, leaving the infantry to press on only to run into more groups of T-34s, which were able to drive almost at will among the bogged down German forces until they ran into the few AA '88s' that had been dragged laboriously forward. Luckily for the Germans the Russians were still tending to use their armour in driblets – there were still not that many T-34s available – and with no infantry support. Their achievement was, therefore, less than it might have been, but the losses so inflicted added to the misery of the ill-supplied German troops, whose lack of preparation for a winter campaign was now showing itself in numerous casualties from cold and sickness as the temperature dropped.

On the flanks of the pierced 'Mozhaisk Line' the Germans were also running into difficulties. The threat of Moscow being outflanked to the north led to the formation of Kalinin Front, under Colonel General Koniev. It consisted of three armies from Zhukov's Front and a special operational group of two rifle and two cavalry divisions with a single tank brigade taken from North West Front and commanded by the latter's Chief of Staff, Lieutenant General Vatutin. As Panzergruppe 3 tried to consolidate its bridgehead over the Volga at the end of October, Koniev pressed in counter attacks supported by newly transferred Siberian armoured brigades. The Germans were driven back and the Russians kept up the pressure: the Germans had to turn loose their Stukas to batter the Russian tanks. Far to the south at Tula, Guderian's 2nd Panzer Army finally got going once more and moved on the town. They were met by strong anti-tank resistance supported by brand new T-34s which successfully held up the armoured half tracks of 3rd Panzer Division. The 50mm guns of the division's *Panzerjäger* battalion were of limited use against the sloped Russian armour. All along the Front, by the end of October, the German advance on Moscow had ground to a standstill. Mud and supply problems were, perhaps, the major causes but the groups of Soviet tanks, especially the wide tracked and heavily protected T-34s wading through the mud and steadily pecking away at the advancing Germans had an important part to play in the Russian successes. Sometimes they caused panic, always they inflicted casualties which the depleted German units, both infantry and armoured, could ill afford to lose. They were a vital piece in the jigsaw of German failure.

The Russians were also eventually managing to frustrate German intentions around Leningrad where Lake Ladoga provided a precarious lifeline to the beleaguered city. In October the Germans began an operation to cut this last access to the outside world by joining up with the Finns east of the Lake. The Russians were already planning an offensive to de-blockade the city and for the westward attack into the Schlusseburg salient 54th Army was reinforced with two tank brigades, 16th and 122nd, to replace the now tankless 21st Tank Division. Between them these brigades could only muster 52 tanks of which 20 were T-34s and KVs but they were better than nothing. To attack from the other direction Major General Fedyuninskii the Leningrad Front Commander had 97 tanks, some 59 of which were KVs. The Germans pre-empted the Russians on the 15th by striking into the weak 4th and 52nd Armies which had little or no armoured support. As the Germans advanced on Tikhvin, whose capture would cut the railway that brought up supplies to the lakeside, forces were drained off from the now cancelled Leningrad offensive; 16th Tank Brigade was put under 4th Army's command. Tikhvin fell on November 12th and Fedyuninskii, transferred to command 54th Army, regained 16th Tank Brigade among other right flank units of the shattered 4th Army, to provide a unified defence of the southern Lodoga shore. At Tikhvin itself Meretskov of

MOSCOW December 1941-April 1942
KEY
Russian Armies
Russian 'Shock' Armies
Russian Cavalry Corps
Russian Partisans
German Armies
German Panzer Armies
German Panzer Groups
Russian attacks
Russian airborne landings
18/24 January 1942
German Counter attacks
Front Lines
5/6 December 1941
1 January 1942
30 April 1942
Moscow Highway
Railways
North West Front
Kalinin Front
West Front
Bryansk Front
(from 18 Dec.)
South West Front
Army Group
North
Army Group Centre
Demyansk
Kholm
Velikiye Luki
Olenino
Rzhev
Belyy
Vitebsk
Demidov
Vyazma
Smolensk
Yelnya
Mogilev
Kirov
Bryansk
Orel
Gomel
Kaluga
Tula
Istra
Moscow
Volga Reservoir
Volga
Lovat
Dvina
Dniepr
Desna
Oka
Don
0
80 m
0
140 km

A T 35 multi-turreted heavy tank. These vehicles were armed with one short 16.5 calibre 76.2 mm gun, two 45 mm high velocity guns and five 7.62 mm DT machine guns. This design was based on the Vickers 'Independent' tanks of the early 1930s. The T 35 had a crew of ten, weighed 45 tonnes, but had an armour protection of only 20-30 mm maximum.

An abandoned Broniford 8-wheel armoured car stands beside a KV-2 during the heavy fighting in central Russia in 1941.

7th Army, who had been holding the Soviet river line against the Finns, took over the Russian defence and in mid November launched a fierce counter attack against the town with tank brigades equipped with precious new T-34s. The Russians suffered heavy casualties – the Germans claimed 50 Soviet tanks destroyed – and only managed to break into the northern outskirts of the town. Nevertheless the Germans were kept at bay and by December had withdrawn from their exposed salient back to the River Volkhov. Leningrad's tenuous line of communication, convoys of trucks driving across the deeply frozen lake, was safe for the winter.

By then the final German lunge at Moscow had been frustrated. The Russians had used the respite given at the beginning of October to consolidate their defending forces. By the time the German offensive opened in mid November the Russians still deployed some 890 tanks, about 100 of these being T-34s and KVs. Nevertheless most formations were pale shadows of their establishments, 58th Tank Division for example had only 350 men and 15 T-26s and BTs. Zhukov noted the preparations for a final offensive and planned limited attacks of his own to disrupt preparations by striking at points of weakness.

One of the biggest of these spoiling counter-attacks was carried out by General Belov's powerful 'Cavalry Mechanised Group', II Cavalry Corps, 415th and 112th Tank Divisions, two more tank brigades and a Katusha rocket regiment against German XIII Corps in 49th Army's area around Serpukhov. This had some effect, the T-34s invulnerability to the 37mm anti-tank gun combined with the attentions of newly arrived Siberian infantry proved too much for the taut morale of the German 112th Infantry Division. The German troops panicked and had to be quickly replaced by fresh units, not a good omen for the forthcoming Moscow offensive.

This was on November 17th. By then its first phase had actually begun across the frozen ground with strong attacks on the northern flank of the Moscow defences below Kalinin. The Russians pushed their tanks into counter attacks, sometimes supporting infantry, sometimes cavalry who were mown down by German artillery and machine-guns. Armour was redeployed from other sectors in vain attempts to stem potential breakthroughs; 145th Tank Brigade was rushed to Zvenigorod to bolster a flagging 5th Army and the vestigial 58th Tank Division was moved north from 16th Army to 30th. On the 23rd the Germans penetrated Solnechnogorsk claiming more than 24 Soviet tanks destroyed in the process, some in a tank v tank combat with 2nd Panzer Division. It was near Solnechnogorsk that the Russians committed their first British tanks, Valentines, still with instructions in Russian chalked on their sides. Unfortunately, due to either shortage of vehicles or tactical ineptitude, these robust little tanks were used in small groups and one such unit, three tanks strong, soon lost two thirds of its strength to an ambush by PzKpfw IV.

Solnechnogorsk fell on the 24th and by then

the whole front west of Moscow had erupted into life. On the 18th 1st Guards Tank Brigade covered the withdrawal of 16th Army from the Chismena area using medium and light tanks in desperate counter-attacks on the advancing Germans. The Brigade retreated through snow covered forests, the tanks and other vehicles sometimes bogging down in the soft going and having to be towed out by others. Katukov was determined not to abandon any as every vehicle counted in the struggle for Moscow. He accompanied his Brigade on foot to help keep up morale and by the 19th his formation had re-formed around Istra and began once more to counter-attack to wear down the advancing enemy.

Guderian began his contribution to the final drive on Moscow on the 18th. His opponent, 50th Army, had an armoured component of only 30 T-26s, all that was left of 108th Tank Division, to support its threatened left flank. The old light tanks vulnerable to every German anti-tank weapon, were soon whittled away. Another 30 Soviet tanks, the combined strength of 11th and 32nd Tank Brigades, fought vainly to hold Venev with an infantry regiment and a militia battalion. Belov's Cavalry Corps was withdrawn from its offensive activity and moved down to fill the hole that had been punched in the Soviet defences. There were problems in bringing up the armour support due to weak bridges but nevertheless Belov was able to form up his men in defensive positions. He was offered two more tank battalions by a grateful Stalin and his II Cavalry Corps was promoted to Guards status. Part of Belov's armoured support, 112th Tank Division, had to be shared with the 49th Army holding the opposite wall of the salient around Serpukhov but Belov tried to form up his part with his two new tank battalions, 35th and 127th and the 9th Tank Brigade in a counter-attack planned to begin on the 27th. Only the 112th's tanks were ready for action on that day to support Belov's cavalry and a heterogenous group of anti-aircraft gunners, sergeant and lieutenant trainees, militia and engineers cobbled together to add their varied weight to the counter-attack. Nevertheless the Germans were forced back three to four kilometres and the two tank battalions and the 9th Tank Brigade were in action by the 28th.

In temperatures that were now down to some 40°C below zero the last days of 1941 saw the line of desperate battles ebb and flow around the western approaches to the Soviet capital. The last reserves of tanks were scraped together to form ad hoc formations such as Major General Lizyukov's 'Group' with a KV company and two rifle brigades or Govarov's 'Mobile Reserve' with 22nd Tank Brigade's 21 tanks and three motor cycle battalions, tasked with holding the junction of 5th and 16th Armies due west of the city. New T-34s produced in factories to the east of Moscow rolled westwards to reinforce the depleted armoured units in action. The Russians were keeping going – just, and an increasingly exhausted Wehrmacht was coming to the end of its tether.

On December 1st the Germans made their last throw, a major attack by 4th Army on the road due west of Moscow. The Soviet 5th Army was now threatened on its northern flank where it joined the 33rd. Another 'composite group', a rifle brigade, some ski troops, a Katyusha unit and two tank battalions was formed out of the available reserves under 33rd Army's commander, Lieutenant General Yefremov. It went into action on December 2nd in the area of Yushkovo and Burtsevo. In a night attack T-34s advanced against the former village where the German soldiers in their summer uniforms were sheltering from the temperatures of -35°C. High explosive tank gun shells and machine-gun fire set fire to the straw roofs of the houses. In the light of the

A BT 7. These tanks were armed with one 45 mm gun with a co-axial 7.62 mm DT machine gun; later models also carried a machine gun in the turret rear and one for AA defence. The BT 7 weighed 13.8 tonnes and had a maximum speed of 73 kph and range of 500 km on the wheels, and 53 kph and 375 km on tracks.

T 26Bs churn through the snow in the winter of 1941. The T 26B was armed with one 46 calibre 45 mm with a muzzle velocity of 816 metres per second. Some models had as many as three 7.62 mm DT machine guns. The T 26B had a range of 375 km on roads and a maximum speed of 28 kph.

burning thatch two Soviet tanks were knocked out by a German '88' but the anti-aircraft gun itself soon succumbed to 76.2mm HE rounds. Three StuG III assault guns were supporting the German infantry and these now duelled with the T-34s among the houses knocking out two. The German infantry gave what help they could with captured Russian anti-tank mines and four more T-34s were destroyed. The Soviet counter-attack was repulsed but the German offensive was also finished. As the Germans withdrew more Soviet tanks appeared and the German officers had to struggle to prevent the retreat turning into a panicked rout. Now it was Soviet armour that had a moral superiority and it was German troops who were suffering from 'tank fear'. By December 6th as the temperature sank to -45°C in places, the Germans had been forced to suspend offensive operations. Two days later Hitler confirmed that the offensive was abandoned.

The desperate exertions of the Red Army; infantry, cavalry, artillery and armour had succeeded. The tactics had not been sophisticated, tanks had been thrown into battle in small units as part of ad hoc formations with no training in combined 'all arms' operations. Yet, as the German losses and shortages wore down the well organised massed armoured formations that Guderian's theories prescribed, the odds grew even. In these conditions of small unit actions the superior design of the new Soviet tanks mattered more than the inexperience of their crews. Yet Soviet tactical expertise was improving. Those who had survived the terrible days of summer and autumn now knew how to exploit the qualities of their mounts both old and new. The Germans were unprepared for a winter campaign but the Russians were more used to its rigours and Finland had taught them many lessons about armoured warfare under the coldest conditions. Armoured sledges had been developed to carry up to 6 - 7 infantrymen towed behind tanks. The broad tracks of the T-34 and KV were just the outward sign of a flexibility that included special prepared oil and fuel and good supplies of anti-freeze for the engine radiators. The Russians knew that keeping a lamp in the engine compartment helped cold starting. Where tanks were left dead for long periods pits were dug underneath in which stoves were emplaced to keep the vehicles warm. The Soviet tank troops were trained when moving through snow not to follow in each other's tracks lest they dig too far in and become stuck. In snowy conditions the best going was found to be hill-crests and other exposed high ground normally avoided by tanks crews. In this respect the Russians' very lack of skill may have helped them.

Now the Soviet counterblow began that Stalin hoped would throw the Germans back from Moscow and perhaps win the war in one decisive campaign. The losses of the past months had been extraordinary. In addition to those already mentioned 212 tanks were lost trying to defend the Donets basin and another 160 when the Crimea was occupied. Total Soviet tank losses had climbed to the staggering figure of 17,000 and the front line tank strength of the Red Army on December 1st, 1941 was only 1,984, less than half the German strength in combat ready tanks and assault guns. It was hoped that the new construction complexes getting under way in the east would soon restore the Soviet tank park to pre-war levels.

A Flawed Offensive

Zhukov had presented his plans for the Moscow counter offensive at the end of 1941. He called for an attack by four armies on the northern German positions around Klin and Solnechnogorsk and by two armies and Belov's reinforced Cavalry Corps on Guderian's southern bulge. Once these had succeeded in driving in the German flanks the four centre armies would go over to the attack to complete the Germans' destruction. Stalin and the General Staff also wished to include Kalinin and South West Fronts to begin "the effective destruction of the enemy" by striking down south west and north west into the German rear with, respectively, three armies and two armies plus an operational group. Zhukov had some 624 tanks for his 600 kilometre front with three tank divisions and 15 tank brigades among 48 rifle divisions, 18 rifle brigades, 3 motor rifle divisions, 15 cavalry divisions and one parachute corps. Of these tanks and formations 14 rifle divisions, 15 rifle brigades, one motor rifle division, 9 cavalry divisions, 1 tank division, 8 tank brigades and 285 tanks were in the first line on the right flank; 16 rifle divisions, one rifle brigade, 2 motor rifle divisions, 5 tank brigades and 194 tanks in the centre and 7 rifle divisions, 5 cavalry divisions, 2 tank divisions, 2 tank brigades and 137 tanks on the left. Koniev's 250 kilometre long Kalinin Front had only two tank battalions and 67 tanks among its 15 rifle divisions, 1 cavalry division and 1 motor rifle brigade. The right wing of Timoshenko's South West Front was even worse off with 2 under-strength tank brigades and a mere 30 tanks among 11 rifle divisions, 1 rifle brigade, 1 motor cycle regiment, 1 motor rifle division and 6 cavalry divisions.

The armoured position in these sectors was hardly overwhelming. An estimated 1,000 German tanks were to be confronted by just 721 Soviet vehicles. Although many German tanks were non-runners many of the Soviet tanks were older BTs and T-26s. Only 185 of Zhukov's tanks were T-34s and KVs and 133 of these were concentrated on his right flank. The strength of individual formations still showed the depleted state of the Red Army's armoured arm; the 112th Tank Division had 86 light tanks, old T-26s and BTs with perhaps an admixture of new T-40s and T-60s, none particularly potent vehicles. 108th Tank Division had only 15 light tanks and 58th Tank Division one T-34 to stiffen 30 T-26s. The Russians had not taken to heart their new tactical instructions and their tanks were still deployed piecemeal. On the central sector of West Front, 33rd Army disposed of its 50 tanks on a basis of 10 tanks per rifle division which meant a density of three vehicles per kilometre. Such were hardly the sophisticated tactics of armoured concentration that would have been necessary to defeat the Wehrmacht under normal circumstances, but the freezing conditions were hardly normal. The German

Two man T 60 light battle tanks in the rubble of Stalingrad. The tank was armed with a 20 mm ShVak automatic cannon and a 7.62 mm machine gun. The 7 hp GAZ-202 six cylinder petrol engine gave a maximum road speed of 42 kph and a range of 235 km. In the background is the earlier model with spoked wheels; in the foreground is a T 60A which had solid wheels and thicker frontal armour.

A T 70 light tank. These vehicles had armour between 40 and 60 mm maximum and a 46 calibre 45 mm gun was mounted with a co-axial DT machine gun. It weighed 9.2 tonnes and its GAZ-202 engines gave a maximum speed of 45 kph and a road range of 350 km.

A section of Soviet infantrymen advance behind a T-34/76B in the first winter of the war in the East. The tank has received a layer of whitewash as camouflage which has rubbed off the top and rear decking.

soldiers, fighting in an alien element at the end of an extended supply line were hardly a difficult target. The conditions did not favour armoured warfare anyway; the ski and the horse were rather more useful means of mobility. Zhukov nevertheless recognised that speed and surprise were vital to make up for the lack of crushing superiority in manpower. He planned to attack weakness not strength and by-pass the centres of heavy resistance. The Germans were about to face a primitive Soviet form of 'winter blitzkrieg'.

The Russian offensive opened even before the Germans had finally abandoned their bid for Moscow. On the 5th of December Kalinin Front struck across the Volga into the left wing of the German bulge around the Volga Reservoir. A few tanks punched holes in the German line through which ski troops pressed into the enemy rear. On the 6th Zhukov launched 30th and 1st Shock Armies in the direction of Klin. Some isolated Soviet tanks were blocked by armoured counter-attacks as the Russians tried primitive frontal attacks. An angry Zhukov, dissatisfied with the slow rate of progress ordered 30th Army to form special mixed combat groups of tanks, infantry and cavalry to strike into the German rear, and destroy their lines of communication. On December 10th Lelyushenko of 30th Army set up such a special 'Mobile Group' under Colonel Chanchibadze. Its tanks (including T-34s), motor riflemen in light trucks, foot soldiers, ski troops and horsemen made considerable gains through the wooded and snow covered territory where the heavier German vehicles with their higher ground pressure could not follow. The Germans mounted counter attacks supported by tanks into the southern flank of 30th Army and these had some success – around Yamuga three T-34s were knocked out and about 1,000 Russians killed or captured on the 9th – but the Soviet advance on both sides of Klin forced its abandonment on the 13th. By then all the northern flank of the Soviet counter attack was in action down to the main Smolensk-Moscow road where 5th Army crashed its 'Shock Group' of mixed infantry and tank units into Panzergruppe 4. The tanks made some penetrations only to meet massed German artillery fire and fierce counter attacks. Here the main advance was made by II Guards Cavalry Corps which succeeded in making penetrations of up to 40 kilometres into the German lines.

On the southern sector the attack against 2nd Panzer Army began on the 6th and 7th. Belov's cavalry, supported by 9th Tank Brigade cut across the German line of retreat. Tank supported ski battalions from 50th Army struck at the retreating Germans who fought back fiercely in combats where poor Soviet tank shooting could still be a decisive disadvantage. The Russians were suffering heavily and 50th Army was soon running out of its limited quota of armour. The Russians were not strong or quick enough to catch the slippery Germans south east of Tula. However the whole German position was threatened when South West Front's 13th Army and Moskalenko's 'Operational Group' (150th Tank Brigade, one cavalry division and one rifle division) hit the German Second Army at Yelets, supported by the 3rd Army to the north around Yefremov. In tanks and motorised sledges the Russians drove the Germans back over 80 kilometres and a gap 30 kilometres wide yawned between the German 2nd Panzer and 4th Armies. Kaluga seemed within the Soviet grasp and with it the way to Vyazma and another encirclement victory, this time a Soviet one. 50th Army formed a special mobile group under Major General V. S. Popov with a rifle division and the light tanks of 112th Tank Division to seize Kaluga. Popov soon got reinforcements in the shape of 131st Tank Battalion, a militia regiment and a cavalry division. By the 20th he was within sight of Kaluga but it took a week's fighting and considerable infantry reinforcement to capture the town. On December 19th Belov was also given 50 more tanks as well as more infantry and cavalry to drive on Yukhnov via Belev with 10th Army in support on his southern flank.

As the southern prong of the Soviet pincers aimed deep in the German rear on the 22nd Koniev's Kalinin Front mounted a major offensive on the northern flank with the main blow aimed at Rzhev. Koniev had been reinforced and his front now had two full tank brigades to support its 30 rifle and 5 cavalry divisions. The new 39th Army had not completed concentrating by H hour but it was able to put two rifle divisions into the attack supported by T-34s. The tanks penetrated the German positions but the enemy infantry were able to keep back their Soviet counterparts with heavy small arms fire. Once isolated the T-34s could be dealt with by artillery or more dangerous means as officers and men climbed onto the rear of Soviet tanks, wedged mines under turrets and pushed small grenades down the gun barrels. The Russians were unable to make an immediate breakthrough even though the full weight of 39th Army was brought to bear. Committed piecemeal it did not get a chance to show its full potential.

The Russians had generally been suffering heavy casualties in the opening weeks of their counter offensive; tank losses had been heavy, 112th Tank Division was down to 15 T-26s and a single T-34 and some tank brigades were reduced to only a single vehicle. Reserves were still limited but Stalin persevered with his ideas for a general counter offensive along the whole front. In addition to completing the destruction of the German forces west of Moscow, Leningrad was to be relieved, Kharkov and the Crimea regained and western bridgeheads captured on the Dniepr across the supply lines of German Army Group South. When Stalin unveiled these plans at a conference on January 5th, 1942, Zhukov pointed to their fundamental flaw, lack of resources; "... for successful operations it is essential to reinforce our forces with men, equipment and to build up reserves, above all tank units, without which we can have no basis for anticipating particular success". Such

A Klementi Vorishilov 1B – an up-armoured model of the KV 1. It had 25 to 35 mm of armour added to bring the total thickness up to 100 mm. It was armed with one 76.2 mm M-1940 (F-34) gun and three DT machine guns and had a crew of five. The 600 hp V-2K diesel engine gave a maximum road speed of 30 kph.

A KV 2 advances through a birch forest in northern Russia. The KV 2 mounted a 20 calibre M-10 152 mm howitzer. An extra loader had to be carried to cope with the heavy ammunition. The armour was 75 mm on the hull and 110 mm on the turret; the total weight was 52 tonnes. Maximum road speed and range were 26 kph and 250 km. These tanks were phased out early in the Russo-German war.

reinforcements did not exist and fuel and ammunition remained in critically short supply. Timoshenko had already asked for 15 new tank brigades for his Kharkov offensive; some of Zhukov's brigades on the vital central sector were lucky to have 15 tanks! Those involved around Moscow strongly recommended concentration of all available resources on this axis and got support from Voznesenskii, co-ordinator of Soviet war production. But Stalin remained adamant: "We must grind the Germans down with all speed so they cannot attack in the Spring".

On January 7th West and Kalinin Fronts got their orders. Kalinin Front was to use a portion of its forces to take Rzhev but also form a 'shock force' containing 'large tank forces' with infantry and cavalry to drive down to Sychevka and Vyazma. Another 'shock group' would be formed by West Front's 1st Guards Cavalry Corps and 50th Army to drive on Vyazma from the south. The aim was nothing less than 'to take prisoner or to annihilate the entire enemy Mozhaisk-Gzhatsk concentration'. Zhukov's centre armies would provide the pressure from the east to hold the German forces while the right flank of 20th Army would co-operate with 30th Army, now transferred to Kalinin Front, in a smaller encirclement around Lotoshino. North West Front and the new Bryansk Front (formed out of the right of South West Front) would cooperate with thrusts in the direction of Rudnya and Orel.

On January 9th North West Front, already heavily committed to the north launched two armies, 3rd Shock and 4th Shock, across the ice of Lake Seliger into the junction of German Army Group Centre and Army Group North. Despite these two Soviet armies' vital role in the proposed encirclement – 4th Shock had been placed under the very senior command of Yeremenko – only a handful of tank units supported their rifle divisions, rifle Brigades and ski battalions. The 4th Shock Army should have had three tank battalions but in the event only deployed two, 141st with four KVs, 6 T-34s and 20 T-60s, 117th with 12 British Matildas ('Mark 2s' as they were known), 9 Valentines ('Mark 3s') and 10 T-60s. With their 20mm armament and 15-20mm protection the T-60s were no more effective than the older Soviet light tanks. Yet to German infantry with no anti-tank guns to hand they were potentially dangerous enough opponents to require the tactics learnt against their heavier cousins. As usual there was little close cooperation on the Soviet side to frustrate such tactics. A line of 8 T-60s from the 141st Tank Battalion attacked the south eastern edge of the village of Okhvat held by a German infantry force. The T-60s directed their automatic cannon and machine-gun fire into the thatched house roofs to deny the Germans shelter and attempted to drive through the village on the direction of Andreapol. A German sergeant climbed on to the back of one little tank, opened the hatch and dropped in an *Eihandgranate* 39 'egg' type grenade; the T-60 blew up. The commander of the second tank opened his hatch to see what was going on and was mown down by a sub-machine gun. A *Stielhandgranate* 24 stick grenade finished off this vehicle. A third tank tried to reverse out of trouble but got stuck in the snow. Again its commander obligingly opened the turret hatch for another German grenade. The five surviving T-60s were thrown into confusion and retreated.

With the Russian tanks partially neutralised by inexperience and tactical ineptitude, the two armies' crack infantry had to bear the brunt of the fighting, achieving a considerable breakthrough. The small groups of armour gave what useful support they could in achieving one or two successes. The Russians grew to respect the tough armour protection of the British infantry tanks even if they found

the lack of a high explosive capability for the 40mm main armament a little frustrating. Nevertheless 61 tanks were not enough for a decisive breakthrough and this reflected a general shortage of equipment and ammunition and even food that could only be made good by ransacking the German stores at Toropets. Six German tanks found here were pressed into service but even these new supplies could not offset the very heavy casualties which had been suffered and the two shock armies ground to a halt in front of Velikiye Luki. 3rd Shock surrounded Kholm but could not take it despite repeated attacks over the following weeks and months. The Russian tanks had to face accurate heavy artillery fire called in from the German lines 10 kilometres away, while one 50mm anti-tank gun available to the defenders also proved a formidable foe. On May 1st 20 rounds from this weapon succeeded in dismissing one group of 5 Soviet tanks and 4 thinly protected T-60s also succumbed to an equally well handled anti-tank rifle.

To the south east the armies of Kalinin Front struck at Rzhev. Again there were very few Russian tanks available and much of the penetration had to be left to unsupported cavalry. Although some horsemen got to the outskirts of Vyazma the Germans were able to make serious counter attacks cutting off the advanced elements of 39th Army. Soviet armour was brought up to support further attacks but the Germans were well emplaced. At Klepenino for example the Der Führer Regiment, SS Motorised Division 'Das Reich'

A T-34/76D, built by the Young Communist League in Khabarovsk, in action in 1942. It has hand rails welded on the turret and rear decking for the tank riders.

Rearming a T 34/76 B in a harbour area in 1942. The T 34/76 B had a welded turret and the long L/41.5 M-1940 76.2 mm gun with new fabricated bolted cradle. The broad tracks gave a low ground pressure and the 500 hp diesel engine had a maximum speed of 53 kph on roads and range of 400 km.

A M3 light tank, part of the Lend Lease equipment given by the United States. The M3 was armed with one 50 calibre 37 mm gun and up to five 7.62 mm machine guns. The tank was powered by a Continental W-670 seven cylinder petrol engine, or a diesel engine.

Far right: A KV-1 rumbles through Gorky Square, Moscow in 1941. Fuel tanks are visible on the tank's hull sides and a steel hawser is attached to the towing links on the tank's bow plate.

deployed one '88' and a number of 50mm and 37mm anti-tank guns as well as 150mm and 75mm infantry guns. A battery of StuG IIIs was in support. The Russians put in a series of manageable, piecemeal assaults, which allowed the Germans in their strong defensive positions to keep them at bay. First came T-34s; the Germans were beginning to get the measure of these now and 50mm anti tank gun crews sought out the weak spots. By February 3rd 20 T-34s had fallen to the 13 available guns of the *Panzerjäger* Battalion 561. Two days later another 4 wrecked Soviet tanks lay in front of the Battalion's positions although one T-34 was able to crush one of the 50mm guns. It was dealt with by infantry with demolition charges and mines. Now 30 light tanks, probably T-60s, closed in to within 50 yards and opened fire with automatic cannon and machine guns. For half an hour the German positions were swept with fire – then the tanks withdrew. One infantry company was wiped out: a breach had been forced in the German line. Yet there was no immediate infantry follow up. It was lucky for the Russians that the non-combatants scraped up to hold the sector soon broke under the strain. Yet in the face of such disorganised Soviet attacks the Germans were eventually able to hold the position. The entire Kalinin Front was now down to a total of about 35 tanks. This was not the force to win a decisive battle of encirclement.

Zhukov's Western Front was also running into trouble in its attempt to drive on Vyazma from east and south east. Vlasov's 20th Army led on Zhukov's right with three tank brigades in his first echelon, supporting two rifle divisions and five rifle brigades. Its task was to punch holes for the following 'breakthrough echelon' based around 2nd Guards Cavalry Corps with three cavalry divisions, five ski battalions and one tank brigade. The first echelon did not concentrate their tanks but again spaced them out so that there were only five or six tanks per kilometre of front. Little advance was achieved and the same was true of 1st Shock Army to the right but 16th Army with 1st Guards Tank Brigade on Vlasov's left made better progress.

There was a new coordination in Russian tactics when the 1st Guards Tank Brigade, 1st Guards Rifle Division and 39th Rifle Division, all under Katukov's central command, struck west from Volokalamsk. The six attached artillery regiments were ordered to keep up with the tanks and infantry to engage targets of opportunity, especially German gun positions, Yet, perhaps partly because self propelled artillery was still not available the fighting eventually degenerated into a slow, attritional affair in which the Soviets suffered heavy casualties and were not able to make a decisive breakthrough. The tank 'ace' Samokhin, among others, was killed. On the 19th a still over confident Stalin weakened the offensive by withdrawing 1st Shock Army to North Western Front. The advance here now ground to a final halt.

On the Smolensk-Moscow motor road Govorov's 5th Army, seven rifle divisions, three rifle brigades, one motor rifle division and 20th Tank Brigade had greater success taking Mozhaisk on the 20th. Again by the end of the month its strength was failing and its neighbouring 33rd Army was cut off by German counter attacks. Further south 43rd Army had dispersed what tanks it had and so had a hard job getting beyond Medyn. 49th Army, with its two tank brigades, six rifle divisions and four rifle brigades had similar problems around Kondorovo. 50th Army was directed at Yukhnov with two rifle divisions, one cavalry division and what was left of 112th Tank Division, while 1st Guards Cavalry Corps was ordered to go straight for Vyazma. This was much to Belov's disgust who believed he had 4th German Army within his grasp if allowed to wheel around Yukhnov towards Medyn and across the German supply lines. Instead he tried to find a suitable path northwards, he succeeded, pushed his corps through, only to be firmly cut off by German counter attacks.

January's fighting around Moscow achieved some major successes for the Red Army, but the decisive victory was still some distance away. Army Group Centre was still intact and not cut off. Indeed several advanced Soviet formations were now in this unenviable position. Paratroops and partisans who were employed to complete the encirclement and link up with the Soviet forces were themselves encircled. Zhukov, since February 1st commander of the whole Western Theatre, was given 200 more tanks for one last try in March. The troops were exhausted, the Spring turned the roads to mud once more and it failed.

What occurred on the Moscow sector was repeated along the whole front as Stalin's over ambitious offensive rolled into motion; some initial success was soon followed by exhaustion and failure. In the north a major new deblockading offensive was planned for Leningrad extending down to the southern shore of Lake Ilmen. Here North West Front's right flank, with the newly created Volkhov Front would swing around into the enemy rear in a major encirclement operation. On the evening of January 7th, without a preliminary artillery bombardment to create maximum surprise, 11th Army opened its attack on Staraya Russa using snow ploughs to clear a path for its KV tanks. These supported the infantry and ski troops, some dropped by glider. Motorised sledges gave the Soviet troops great mobility and considerable penetrations were obtained. Staraya Russa was soon completely surrounded, but it proved difficult to take like other isolated strongpoints to the east such as Vzvad, held by a mixed bag of 543 German troops ranging

T 34/76 C tanks on the move. These vehicles were introduced in early 1942. Among the improvements were an armoured shield to the hull machine gun. Performance was similar to that of the T 34 A and a crew of four remained the same for the four variants.

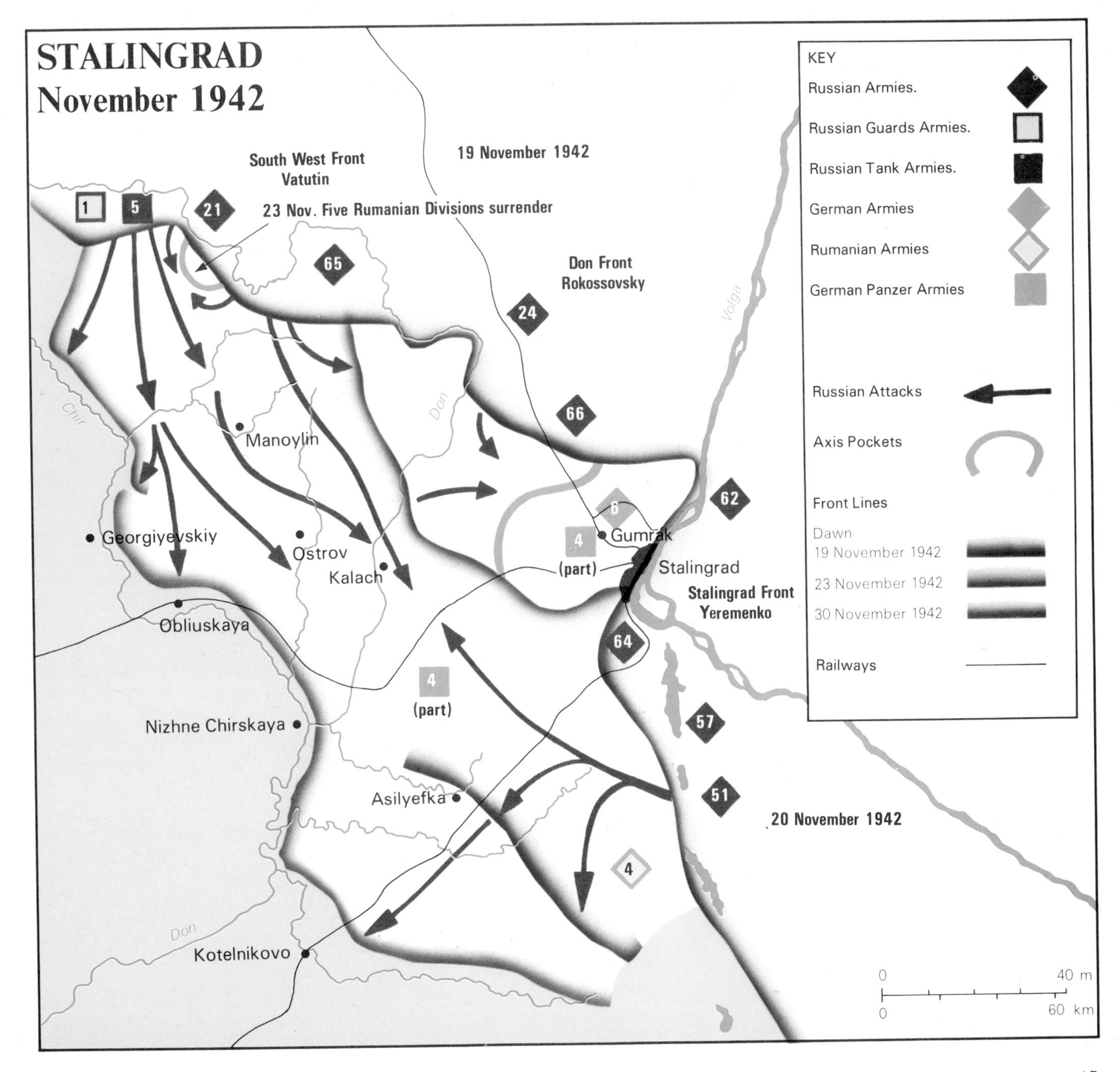
STALINGRAD
November 1942
KEY
Russian Armies.
Russian Guards Armies.
Russian Tank Armies.
German Armies
Rumanian Armies
German Panzer Armies
Russian Attacks
Axis Pockets
Front Lines
Dawn 19 November 1942
23 November 1942
30 November 1942
Railways
South West Front
Vatutin
19 November 1942
23 Nov. Five Rumanian Divisions surrender
Don Front
Rokossovsky
Stalingrad Front
Yeremenko
20 November 1942
1
5
21
65
24
66
62
6
4
(part)
64
57
51
Volga
Don
Chir
Manoylin
Georgiyevskiy
Ostrov
Kalach
Gumrak
Stalingrad
Obliuskaya
Nizhne Chirskaya
Asilyefka
Kotelnikovo
0
40 m
0
60 km

from *Panzerjägers* to Luftwaffe signallers. The tactics the Russians adopted to reduce this strongpoint show the lack of a coordinated 'all arms' approach that was such a weakness of the Red Army at this time. Over several days ski troops, then Katyusha rockets, then air attacks and finally tanks were all thrown separately at the German lines. The Russians tried night assaults in which one T-26 was able to penetrate the German positions but, worried by grenade attacks, it was eventually dismissed by two well placed anti-tank rounds. A fiercer night attack five days later cost four more light tanks to grenade attacks. Only after 13 days were the Germans forced to break out westwards.

Although the Russians were able to cut away 'pockets' of German resistance, notably around Demyansk, they had enormous difficulty in reducing them. The offensive soon stalled and Volkhov and Leningrad Fronts' attacks to the north did no better when they began on the 13th. The Russians smashed in their usual disorganised way against strong German positions. A regiment of KVs was switched from Leningrad over the ice of Lake Ladoga to reinforce 54th Army as it battered its way westwards. Only on the 24th did Volkhov Front's 2nd Shock Army obtain a breakthrough and pushed mixed groups of tanks, infantry and cavalry into the German rear. Despite severe communications and supply problems 2nd Shock advanced about 90 kilometres in just over a week and swung round on Lyuban to meet 54th Army coming down from the north. To speed the breakthrough here the 54th were given further reinforcement in the shape of 4th Guards Rifle Corps, one rifle division, four rifle brigades, three ski battalions, a Katyusha group and a tank brigade. 54th Army got within 25 kilometres of 2nd Shock but the pincers did not meet. The latter was in a chaos of disorganisation as incompetent staff officers grappled with the problems of keeping extended mechanised forces going far behind enemy lines. 2nd Shock's Chief of Operations and Chief of Staff were both dismissed and its commander, Klykov, fell ill under the strain and was replaced by Lieutenant General Vlasov. Air support was very limited and there was just not enough armour to push the advance forward at any speed. The Russians were trying a 'blitzkrieg' with insufficient resources of expertise or power. Guderian had always insisted that deep penetrations had to be made in width as well as depth. Despite attempts to widen the Soviet corridor it remained perilously narrow and on March 19th the predictable happened, a German counter attack cut straight through it. On the 27th Vlasov was able to use his armour to regain contact but his army remained terribly exposed in an area that would become an impossible marsh when the Spring thaw came.

Down in the south five tank brigades had supported the recapture of Rostov at the end of November 1941 and it was now planned to land two Soviet armies, 44th and 51st, on the Kerch Peninsula to create a new Crimean beachhead. A little armoured support was provided. 44th Army's Group A had 34 tanks to support the 23,000 men directed against Feodosiya on the south side of the peninsula on December 29th. Group B brought in another nine. Most, if not all, of these seem to have been T-26s which were powerful enough to drive off the Rumanian Mountain Corps tasked with driving the Russians back into the sea. They were not quick enough, however, to stop the Germans preparing a defensive line across the neck of the peninsula. When they attacked it they were successfully held off. One group of T-26s was engaged by StuG III assault guns at a range of 600 metres. Outgunned and outfought the Soviet light tanks, although superior in numbers, were forced to retreat leaving behind 16 knocked out vehicles. There had been some Soviet success – the Germans had been forced to withdraw from the Kerch Peninsula and the pressure had been taken off the siege of Sevastopol – but the new 'Crimea Front' had been contained.

The Southern Offensive which had begun so well around Rostov had stalled at the Donets by the end of December. Again Soviet failure could be accounted for by poor use of armour. This is illustrated by an action fought north east of Lisichansk by the German Infantry Regiment 203. Here Soviet 2nd Army deployed three rifle divisions, a cavalry division and a partly T-34 equipped tank brigade in an attempt to break through around the village of Berestovaya. On the 22nd the Russians attacked with infantry alone and only belatedly employed tanks when their first attempts failed. On the evening of the 23rd to the left of the Lisichiansk road an attack by two rifle divisions supported by ten tanks had little artillery support and little more success. It was met by concentrated German artillery fire and the Soviet armour, split away from the infantry, was forced into retreat. The German infantry were quite easily able to repulse the unsupported Soviet riflemen. Christmas Eve saw more infantry attacks but none accompanied by tanks. After more failures the Russians pushed in their tanks again on Christmas Day with about a dozen advancing slowly through the snow on the village's western flank. They were accompanied by infantry and supported by heavy artillery and mortar fire. With the tanks' guns shooting up troublesome German defensive positions the Russians were able to penetrate the village with five vehicles. Now, however, the tanks and infantry separated and this gave the outnumbered Germans a chance to get their anti-tank gunners into action. Two of the Russian tanks were knocked out and the rest retreated.

On the 26th about three rifle battalions renewed the offensive, supported by some 17 tanks, to the west of Berestovaya. They had some success in crushing defensive positions before being stopped by artillery. To the left one tank was knocked out by an 88mm battery but the Russians were eventually able to deal with this difficult obstacle with high explosive counter fire. The Soviets cut off the Germans in the village from the Regimental H.Q. in Belgorovka to the south west. The Germans were now considering withdrawal but were still able to keep at bay frontal attacks directed against Berestovaya. The Germans were using assault guns in support of the infantry. Eventually on the 27th coordinated attacks using T-34s which were able to stand up to the German 37mm anti tank guns finally dislodged the Germans from the village. The wide tracks of the T-34s enabled them to out manoeuvre the StuG IIIs. Yet Russian strength had been worn down in these piecemeal assaults and the Soviets were unable to press on. Throughout the battle the Russians had shown a remarkable reluctance to use their tanks en masse or to properly coordinate all arms in a decisive assault. The extra mobility conferred by the wide tracked and heavily protected T-34s was only very belatedly used to out manoeuvre the Germans and was wasted in slogging away in unsophisticated frontal attacks. Only after considerable losses in men and equipment was sufficient strength used to obtain a success but this could not be exploited due to the earlier losses.

These problems of wasteful incompetence had not been solved when the Russians once more tried to drive over the Donets in January. Some gains were made in the Oboyan-Kursk area by 21st and 40th Armies at the beginning of the month. Directly in front of Kursk a group of 25 T-34s with 'tank descents' of infantry riding on them skilfully exploited a gap between two German regiments and drove on through the snow. Two or three battalions of infantry came up in support to safeguard the flanks of the penetration. When the Russians had got to within about ten kilometres of Kursk a German Panzer battalion carried out a flanking counter attack and took the village of Vybolsova, so cutting off the Soviet spearheads. Placing their faith in tank proof country the Germans deployed their PzKpfw III and IV and an 88mm anti-aircraft gun to cover all the major lines of approach. A first counter attack from the west was thus quickly driven off, but the T-34s soon showed the Germans that 'tank proof' was a relative term with the Soviet tanks' better ground clearance and lower ground pressure. A two pronged attack quickly retook Vybolsova and the road block was smashed. Nevertheless some delay had been caused as German resistance solidified and the advance slowed to a standstill later in the month.

Now 38th, 6th, 57th and 37th Armies opened a new offensive aimed at Kharkov and the Dniepr. Although the advance of 38th Army on Kharkov was soon halted between Balakleva and Slavyansk a penetration about 130 kilometres wide was made in the German line by Soviet tanks and infantry. The heavy break-through fighting involved more casualties and, while another whole army, 9th, moved up, a request was made to Moscow for more reinforcements. As Stalin saw the opportunity for the encirclement of Army Group South's right wing no less than 315 more tanks were sent to give more armoured weight. By the end of January about ten tank brigades were engaged in helping gouge out a major bulge in the German line, but there was never sufficient concentration of force for a really decisive breakthrough in the network of defensive strongpoints that dotted the snow covered countryside. Tanks were again widely spread out in support of infantry units. Between January 10th and April 7th the German divisions south of Kharkov repulsed 142 attacks and knocked out 42 tanks, a monument to both Soviet persistence and the limited strength of the individual assaults.

Here and there slightly more powerful groups of new tanks were able to achieve some effect, such as on February 11th when 11 KV-1s were grouped with a battalion of infantry to attack through the thawing mud towards Yakovenkovo, north of Balakleva. Counter attacks by German tanks were beaten off by the 76.2mm fire of the Soviet armour and the Germans were forced back. Again, however, the Russians chose to delay and allowed the enemy to build up new defences under intermittent shellfire from tanks, artillery and Katyushas. Eventually on the 14th and 15th the Russians threw themselves against these positions, which were by now strong enough to repulse the mixed Soviet groups. By this time the Russian offensive had ground to a halt all around the Izyum 'bulge'.

All was not well in the Crimea either for Manstein mounted a major counter offensive in the middle of January, pre-empting Soviet plans for an offensive of their own. The limited Soviet tank strength was destroyed as 85 vehicles were knocked out or captured. Now the Red Army began to reinforce Crimea Front and by the end of January two tank brigades were available for action. These had new T-34s and to supervise their use Mekhlis, Stalin's personal representative, ordered down General B.T. Volskii, Inspector General of Armoured Forces and the Commander of the Soviet Union's first mechanised brigade. The Soviet offensive was delayed until the end of February and the Russians pressed into the attack on the 27th with tank supported infantry columns. The thaw softened the ground and heavy German artillery fire added to Soviet problems. The Russian formation commanders spread their armour across the front and Volskii, who had wanted the attack delayed to build up more strength, had a hard time persuading them to adopt a more sophisticated approach. Repeated attacks in March remained stalled with heavy losses – the Germans claimed 136 tanks knocked out in the period 13th to 16th March alone – but the Germans were also being ground down and Manstein had to launch the new 22nd Panzer Division into the attack to shore up his line. This met preparations for a further Soviet attack and sustained heavy losses but the next wave of Soviet attacks, beginning on March 26th, were also reduced in strength. On April 9th a final Soviet attempt was made to break through into the Crimea by 44th and 51st Army with six rifle divisions supported by 150 tanks – to be once more stopped dead.

By this time the failure of Stalin's grand design was plain to see. The General Staff recommended going over to a 'provisional strategic defensive' although the ever aggressive Stalin favoured new 'partially offensive operations' to wear down German strength. Zhukov again opposed these plans stressing the need to build up Soviet strength for a new major offensive in more favourable conditions. There had just not been enough supplies or equipment to carry out the ambitious plans of the past winter. The shortage of tanks was only one of a whole series of deficiencies, although perhaps the most important in view of armour's dominance of the modern battlefield. What tanks there were had often been wasted, spread out both strategically and tactically and badly supported by infantry and artillery. The speed with which the 'Stalin Offensive' had been planned put an extra strain on troops who were still largely novices in the art of armoured warfare. Such men required detailed planning and orders; they could not respond to the unknown like their mature German counterparts. This was especially true when only a few tanks had radios and the whole Soviet system of tactical communications remained primitive and inflexible. Knocking out commander's tanks meant that whole platoons and companies could be neutralised and cut off from higher authority. The Germans were always ready to exploit any favourable chink in the Soviet armour and many a Soviet platoon commander must have been killed having to expose himself to make the necessary flag signals to organise his subordinates.

At least, however, the T-34s and KVs had favourable technical qualities to set against these shortcomings. The unfortunate crews of the older BTs and T-26s had no such protection and still bearing the brunt of a good deal of the fighting these tanks became death traps. Although their unfortunate crews referred to their mounts having guns 'only fit for shooting sparrows' BTs or T-26s were not, in objective terms, hopelessly inferior. In more skilled hands they might still have proved adequate armoured vehicles, even in 1941-42: but 10 - 25mm armour could provide no simple answer to the problem of getting an inaccurately fired, medium length 45mm gun into an effective position. Soviet crews needed simpler solutions, as provided by the T-34s and KVs coming off the production lines in encouragingly large numbers. By the Spring of 1942 the older tanks were fast disappearing from the battlefront although they remained in service in the Far East until 1945. If the new vehicles were conserved for better prepared offensives all might yet be well for the Russians – but would the Germans give them the chance?

The Price of Experience

1942 saw Soviet tank production well under way as the eastern factories swung into action and productivity rose by some 38 per cent. The finer points of finish and quality were sacrificed to provide the necessary numerical superiority on which victory depended. In the first half of the year 11,177 Soviet tanks left the production line, more than the total German production of tanks since the beginning of 1939! Of this total 4,414 were T-34s: plans for a radically modified medium were sensibly shelved. Only the turret of the new tank was gradually adapted on new production T-34s as it overcame a number of serious tactical problems of the old design. The clumsy, single turret hatch had proved difficult to look round with any degree of safety and it also created a large hole in the top through which grenades could be lobbed. It was replaced by two smaller hatches, one for the commander and one for the loader. The new turret also dispensed with the vulnerable rear overhang, so useful as a place to wedge mines and other explosive charges. There were at least two versions of this basic design as variety became a confirmed feature of Soviet tank production. With up to 42 production plants of differing degrees of sophistication turning out variations on the T-34 (and KV) themes, numerous detail differences became apparent. None was important enough to create logistics difficulties but they posed problems of nomenclature with which German intelligence bravely grappled.

Heavy tanks accounted for 1,663 vehicles as production of the clumsy KV-2 was abandoned, plans for an up-armoured 85mm armed KV-3 were also shelved and resources were concentrated on the more than adequate KV-1. By now this almost impregnable tank was acquiring even heavier armour of up to 120 - 130mm total thickness, increasing still further its invulnerability to German anti-tank weapons.

The light tank still formed an important part of Soviet armoured strength due to its ready availability from the car and truck industry. Some 5,100 completed the balance of January - June 1942 production. Some T-40 amphibious tanks continued to be produced, but to improve the limited combat capabilities of the T-60 a new T-70 appeared with thicker armour and a 45mm gun. With some anti-tank potential the new tank was a considerable advance on its predecessor but was still not an enviable machine for an over worked two man crew on an increasingly dangerous battlefield. Although the Russians had been impressed by the German StuG III assault guns there was, as yet, no direct Soviet equivalent – although 57mm anti tank guns were now put on the little Komsomolets chassis to provide SU-57 tank destroyers.

Progress was also being made in the development of larger, armoured formations. From March tank corps began to be formed

Far left: T-34/76Fs on a production line in a factory in the Urals in 1943. By moving their production centres to the Urals the Russians put these factories out of the range of bombers and advancing German ground forces. After some early dislocation these plants were soon mass producing tanks on a vast scale.

by grouping three tank brigades with a motor rifle brigade, a reconnaissance battalion and a motor cycle battalion. These deployed about 180 tanks and four I, III, IV and XVI were sent to Bryansk Front in April. Each had 88 T-34s, 24 KV-1s and 69 T-60s. Tank corps were soon being grouped, with some extra formations, into tank armies, the first two of which, 3rd and 5th were formed in May - June. All fully mechanised tank armies were 'homogenous', those with ordinary rifle divisions were 'mixed establishment'. Tank corps and tank armies were relatively crude attempts to maximise the shock power of armour but both were 'tank heavy' and contained a low proportion of other echelons. They were insufficiently well balanced formations for real mobile warfare on the German pattern and tended to be used as sources of tank brigades for dispersed NPP work among the rifle divisions. It was indeed accepted doctrine that this should be done during the breakthrough phase of operations before formations were reassembled for exploitation. In January Stavka ordered that tank brigades should be committed in full strength with the full cooperation of infantry, air and artillery and with proper reconnaissance. This was another step in the right direction, yet much had still to be learnt about the nature of armoured operations, notably the dangers of strategic and tactical dispersion. This was shown by the fate of Timoshenko's 'limited Kharkov offensive' which jumped off on the 12th May. Stalin liked Timoshenko's idea of attacking and had not been sparing with armour. Two new tank corps, XXI and XXIII and about 850 other tanks supported 640,000 men from South Western and Southern Fronts. The strategy was a repetition of the 'Stalin Offensives' with 28th Army this time striking from Volchansk in the north east and 6th Army coming up out of the existing Izyum 'bulge' to the south. The 'bulge' itself was to be extended westwards to Krasnograd on the Kharkov-Dnepropetrovsk railway. Southern Front would secure the southern flank of the 'bulge' with 57th and 9th Armies. Thirteen NPP tank brigades were available, ten in the front line but the spreading of these on the basis of one per rifle division meant tank concentrations of only 3 – 8 per kilometre and limited the force of the offensive. Nevertheless some gains were made and it seemed a breakthrough was possible. 6th Army advanced 25 kilometres and 28th Army 20. Timoshenko, southern area supreme commander, personally directed South Front and deployed XXI Tank Corps as a concentrated exploitation force for just this eventuality. He was reluctant to commit it however due to fears of meeting German armour mistakenly reported south of Kharkov. He finally made up his mind on March 17th but on that day real German tanks, brought up from 1st Panzer Army went into action. Despite bringing down first single tank brigade and then both his tank corps to hold the line, the Soviet formations were deployed piecemeal and out fought. By May 22nd the Izyum 'bulge' had been cut off. Fanatical breakout attempts by Soviet infantry, supported by tanks, had some success but were finally halted. 6th and 57th Armies were trapped and destroyed and the Germans claimed 1,250 Soviet tanks, captured or knocked out.

More tanks were lost further south after Manstein went over to the offensive in the Crimea on May 8th. The Crimean Front now disposed of three armies, supported by four tank brigades. One of these was attacked on May 9th as 22nd Panzer Division broke through east of Feodosia and, taken by surprise, was easily dispersed. The incompetence of Mekhlis, Deputy Defence Commissar and Stavka Representative, coupled with complete German command of the air, prevented a proper Soviet response to the highly mobile

German advance. Russian tanks did mount some quite heavy counter attacks on 22nd Panzer but they were not strong enough and were repulsed. An evacuation by sea was prevented by German artillery fire and after ten days 258 more defunct Soviet tanks littered the Kerch peninsula. A month later, to the north another 170 vehicles were found in the marshes west of the Volkhov as 2nd Shock Army was cut off and destroyed – despite the efforts of 29th Tank Brigade which cut a short-lived 400 metre path to the beleaguered army after a week of heavy fighting. On June 25th all attempts of getting 2nd Shock out had been defeated.

Three days later, the main German summer offensive opened, aimed at Stalingrad and the oilfields of the Caucasus. Stalin had refused to believe that such an offensive was coming, and was planning another 'limited offensive' around Orel. On June 28th, however, reality struck the Soviet lines west of Voronezh in the shape of 4th Panzer and 2nd Army. Golikov, commander of Bryansk Front, not unduly surprised himself, moved up I and XVI Tank Corps to the River Kshen. A considerably more surprised Stavka moved in two more Tank Corps, IV and XXIV, from South West Front, together with XVII Tank Corps from its own reserve. One of the first of the new tank armies, 5th, with II and XI Tank Corps was also brought up. A mighty concentration of over 1,200 KV-1s, T-34s, T-60s and T-70s was now available to check the German breakthrough, although the Soviet signals system was already beginning to collapse. Golikov had already lost contact with IV and XXIV Tank Corps. Stalin gave strict instructions on the employment of this mass of armour and sent Federonko, the Soviet chief of armoured forces, to supervise in person. Stalin ordered Golikov to concentrate on the German spearheads rather than their flanks, and Stavka continued to bombard the Front commander with a stream of exhortations, admonitions and orders on his conduct of armoured operations. The unfortunate general only had a weak radio link to the armoured 'command centre' at Kastornoye, where Fedorenko had no staff or signals system to control the scattered tank corps. It was not quite clear if Golikov was instructing Fedorenko or the other way round. Eventually on July 1st the General Staff told Golikov to accept Fedorenko's orders on armoured operations.

In these circumstances it was hardly surprising if the Soviet armoured counter attacks lacked muscle. XVII and XXIV Tank Corps took time to get moving IV Tank Corps only engaged with a few advanced battalions. By the 3rd July the Germans were over the Don near Voronezh and IV, XVII and XXIV Tank Corps fell back on the town. Colonel General Vasilevskii, new Chief of General Staff, tired of orders at long range came down to personally supervise a counter attack by 5th Tank Army from its concentration area south of Yelets into the flank of the German advance. However Major General Lizyukov, the Army commander, bungled the attack. Instead of committing his 360 or so tanks in massed brigades, they were disposed in long columns only the leading ends of which were engaged at any one time by the Germans. As these relatively manageable groups of armour were held, the Luftwaffe got to work on the rest of the column. Air attacks split the Soviet armour up still further and destroyed what little organisation the Russians had been able to build up.

These opening battles proved that there was more to defeating the Panzers, and the Wehrmacht in general, than just forming tank corps and armies. The new larger formations posed problems of command and control which had not yet been solved. Without proper reconnaissance the Russians were usually at least one step behind the Germans and were never able to recapture the initiative. Tanks were still split up to support rifle units fighting an all too static defence. It was no use deploying more tanks than the Germans, who had only two Panzer and three motorised infantry divisions in 4th Panzer Army, if the Germans were always able to exploit local superiority. German shooting and general tank handling remained superior.

On June 30th, the German 6th Army began its advance eastwards to link up with 4th Panzer Army to the north and to drive down the west bank of the Don, threatening to cut off Southern and South Western Fronts in a major battle of encirclement. The Russians were pushed back from July 9th by the advance of 1st Panzer and 17th Armies, whom the Germans saw as the southern prong of their double envelopment. However they had finally learned some of their lessons and began to fall back over the Don out of danger. As the units of South Western Front streamed back to the Don in some confusion, measures were taken to stiffen the defence of the river line and to keep at least some of the territory within its bend in Soviet hands. On July 12th a new Stalingrad Front was formed from three reserve armies. By the 22nd the new Front could muster 360 tanks, less than half the 740 estimated to be on the strength of Paulus's reinforced 6th Army. Attempts were begun to form some 'mixed establishment tank armies' out of two of South West Front's armies battered after the breakthrough battles and disorganised by their retreat. 38th Army became 1st Tank Army in the Don bend itself, with XII and XXVIII Tank Corps, 158th Tank Brigade and 131st Rifle Division. 28th Army was converted into 4th Tank Army and held back over the Don with XXII and XXIII Tank Corps, 133rd Tank Brigade, 18th Rifle Division and a number of artillery regiments. It took time to form up and equip these formations since they were very short of both men and armour. Nevertheless they constituted the only available counter attack reserve.

Fuel problems in 6th Army gave Stalingrad Front a welcome respite before Paulus attacked into the Don bend from July 17th. At first 62nd and 64th Armies, managed to hold out, but on July 23rd the Germans began to make progress as armoured forces jabbed into the flanks of the Soviet defences. The right wing of 62nd Army, together with its tank brigade, was encircled by the northern German pincer which had fought through to the Don. 64th Army tried to bring some of its armour across the river to shore up its junction with 62nd but was forced back on the river in some panic.

Now seemed to be the time to commit the tank armies and Vasilevskii himself was once again sent down to supervise. 4th Tank Army was to be brought over the Don at Kachalinskaya and would strike westwards to join with 1st Tank Army coming up from Kalach in 62nd Army's rear. The German penetration to the Don would be pinched out and the already encircled Soviet forces relieved. Unfortunately the two armies were far from ready, 4th could only deploy one under-strength tank corps, XXII with no more than 80 tanks. 1st Tank Army, already over the river, was in rather better shape with both its tank corps and its rifle division, but again 160 tanks was a meagre total for six tank brigades. As speed was essential Major General Moskalenko's 1st Tank Army began its attack on the 27th even though it was realised that 4th Tank Army could only get into motion the next day. The Luftwaffe battered the advancing tanks, knocking out a few, but more importantly, blowing headquarters and signals systems to pieces, making proper command and control impossible. It was very difficult for XXII Tank Corps to get its armour over the river and by the late afternoon of the 27th only 14 vehicles were across. A few more were across by 03.00 the next morning, the assigned jump-off time, but not enough to make much impression against XIV Panzer Corps' left flank. Moskalenko's XIII Tank Corps was making rather better progress from the Kalach direction as the encircled portion of 62nd Army threw its armour into an attempt to join up with the advancing spearheads. The dusty steppes of the Don Bend, excellent tank country, were seeing a classic tank battle as the various armoured formations, Soviet and German, manoeuvred to secure positions of advantage. The Russian strength was about half T-34 and KV although their tank units were also leavened by heavily protected British built Matildas and the first 'lend-lease' American tanks. The M3AI lights soon became popular with their crews due to their better control, manoeuvrability and reliability compared with Soviet armour, as well as the accuracy of their armament. Less popular were the larger M3 mediums with their hull-mounted 75mm guns, large crew and high silhouette. They were soon nicknamed 'incinerators for seven persons' by the Soviet tank crews.

The Russians showed some tactical improvement during this fighting in which the Germans excelled with their good control and accurate fire. The Russians were now having to face not only new, longer-gunned PzKpfw III and IV but new 75mm anti-tank guns and even their own 76.2mm guns, captured and pressed into service as a ready means of opening up T-34s. These new tanks and anti-tank weapons diminished the margin of superiority of the T-34 and KV-1 and put even the noticeable, but limited, Soviet tactical improvements at a discount. The Russians were 'having to run to stand still' in armoured warfare techniques and the extra emphasis on enhanced tactical expertise was something with which the Soviet armoured forces could not cope. Soon the sandy plains were covered with more wrecked Soviet tanks than German. Sometimes the Russians were able to lay tank ambushes and succeed in cutting off German detachments and inflicting casualties, but in general the Germans had command of the situation. As pressure on the southern flank of the Soviet line increased XXIII Tank Corps was brought down to support 64th Army hanging on to its bridgeheads north of the Chir but this only weakened 4th Tank Army's counter offensive without saving the situation south of Kalach. By the end of July 1st Tank Army had been brought to a halt and a few days later the three tank corps in the Don Bend were down to 15-20 operational tanks each. Final, ill coordinated counter attacks with such limited forces were very easily dealt with and by the 8th the Germans succeeded in completely encircling 62nd Army and 1st Tank Army. When the 'pocket' was finally liquidated 270 Soviet tanks were found either knocked out or captured.

By now a new danger had arisen for the Russians. If the sacrifice of the tank armies had done nothing else they had alerted Hitler to the fact that Stalingrad was heavily defended. 4th Panzer Army, originally intended for Stalingrad, had been diverted to the lower Don in order to give extra weight to the drive on the Caucasus, which had now taken Hitler's fancy. Now, at the end of July, it was redirected north eastwards to relieve pressure on the apparently flagging 6th Army. To deal with the danger Yeremenko was given command of South East Front carved out of the southern wing of Stalingrad Front. His staff was set up from the 1st Guards Tank Army's command echelon and the survivors of XIII Tank Corps remained with Stalingrad Front, which also had 4th Tank Army's survivors holding the strip of territory between the Volga and the Don. In all, on August 15th, Stalingrad Front had some 200 tanks left to back its 26 divisions and South East only 70 for its 16. By then Yeremenko had been given over-all command of both fronts.

Yeremenko had some success in delaying the advance of 4th Panzer Army but on August 15th the Germans began their concerted attempt to take Stalingrad. The remnants of XXII Tank Corps were quickly driven back on the Don, leaving a trail of knocked out tanks in their wake. By the 21st 6th Army had crossed the Don and there was precious little Soviet armour available to mount counter attacks. Three new tank corps were among the reinforcements Stavka were sending to bolster the Stalingrad defence but they had little chance to deploy when 16th Panzer Division burst out of its Don bridgehead on the 23rd and reached the Volga. Steps were quickly taken to deal with this incursion. One of the new corps, II, together with XXIII Tank Corps, partially rebuilt with new or repaired tanks from Stalingrad's Dzherzhinski Tractor Works, was to strike north of Rynok at the tip of the German penetration. This attack was commanded by Shtevnev, chief of the Front's armoured and mechanised troops. On its left the re-assembled 62nd Army would strike north to meet the XXVIII Tank Corps and three infantry divisions supported by an independent tank brigade striking southwards. Though the tanks were still employed in small groups this latter operation, which began during the night, had some success and the two forces linked up. Unfortunately, Shtevnev's attack, planned for the 24th, ran into 16th Panzer's own assault on the northern suburb of Spartakovka and had a more difficult time. As in Leningrad only a few months before some of the new tanks were unpainted and driven by scratch crews of tank constructors. A few even lacked gunsights and were only able to make small penetrations into the German lines before being knocked out.

By September 14th there were only 120 tanks in the area of 62nd and 64th Armies. Brigades were down to only 10 vehicles each, corps to less than 50. Counter attacks from the north, supervised by Zhukov himself, drew off some German forces but on September 13th a major German attack on Stalingrad began. Soviet tanks were effectively dug in up to their turrets as well camouflaged anti-tank defences 200 - 300 metres behind the Russian front line. The Soviets let the Germans get into unfavourable positions and then opened fire in ambush. Two tank brigades of 30 T-34s between them, together with two anti-tank regiments held off many times their number of German vehicles. The Germans were forced to stop using their tanks en masse but in small mixed battle groups with heavy air and artillery support, better suited to the restricted city conditions.

One skeleton tank brigade retook the Barrikady and Krasnyi Oktyabr factories after they fell to the German assault detachments but despite heavy counter attacks the Germans got within 800 metres of 62nd Army's H.Q. on the 14th. Its new commander, Chuikov, brought in his last reserve brigade of 19 T-34s. The nature of the armoured warfare in the city is shown by the brigade's orders; three vehicles were to knock out German machine gunners holed up in the engineer's house, a battalion of six was to block the streets leading from the railway station to the landing stage. By dusk only one of those tanks was still in action, although it had been disabled and could not move. The surviving men of the brigade, no more than about 100, were ordered to assemble round the T-34 and fight on. Half were soon dead but infantry reinforcements now came across the Volga to reinforce the crumbling Soviet positions. 62nd Army held on – just.

On the 17th in answer to Chuikov's call for more reserves 137th Tank Brigade from II

Tank Corps was ferried across with T-70s, which were relatively easy to take over the fire-swept Volga on the available transport. The little tanks deployed about 600 metres north east of 62nd Army's H.Q. and helped hold the line against the repeated German attacks towards the Volga. Meanwhile three full tank corps were preparing to re-open the attempt of Stalingrad Front to break through the German cordon north of the city. Originally timed for the 17th the attack went in at 05.30 on the 18th with two of the tank corps supporting the first wave of infantry. These hurriedly assembled formations were largely composed of T-60s and T-70s, which were no match for the PzKpfw III and IV which surged in to meet them; 50mm and 75mm rounds made the outgunned little Russian vehicles 'burn like candles' and the 45mm guns of the T-70s could make only a limited response. Stukas from Fliegerkorps VIII added their weight to the German counterblow, attacking the massed groups of 30-40 light tanks. As the accompanying infantry went to ground the attack was literally stopped in its tracks with groups of wrecked T-60s and T-70s testifying to the patent obsolescence of an armoured concept.

On the 19th the Germans launched a three sided attack on the heights of Mamayev Kurgan with over 40 PzKpfw III and IV. They were faced by five T-34s and three T-60s. One of the T-34s, commanded by Sergeant Major Smekhotvorov, knocked out two German tanks. As the crews jumped out they were machine gunned down and the rest of the demoralised Germans retreated. Yet by the 26th most of the southern part of the city was in German hands and 62nd Army was cut off from 64th. Stavka, concerned for greater things, left only a trickle of reinforcements going into the city, just enough for Chuikov to hold on.

Still the Soviet perimeter slowly contracted. By early October the Tractor Plant itself was itself a scene of bitter fighting after being heavily bombed by Fliegerkorps VIII. Now it was decided to send in more tanks and Colonel Bely's 84th Tank Brigade was chosen with its 5 KVs, 24 T-34s and 20 T-70s. Again, at first, only the T-70s could be got across the river and they were rushed up to act as pillboxes in support of 37th Guards Rifle and 308th Rifle Divisions defending the Tractor Plant. Eventually the heavier armour was brought across the Volga on larger barges crammed with extra ammunition and the brigade helped beat off an attack on October

Loading T-40 amphibious tanks in September 1941. The T-40 had a top speed of 27½ mph on land and 4 mph in water, It was armed with a 12.7 mm or 20 mm D.Sh.K. and a co-axial DT machine gun.

7th by two infantry divisions and an estimated 150 German tanks. Some 16 German tanks were lost to 3 Russian. Nevertheless Bely's Brigade was soon reduced to 20 vehicles.

By the 9th there were still 80 tanks in 62nd Army to pit against the Germans' estimated 300. Some were still capable of being used in a mobile role. One mixed group, three tanks and an 18 man infantry platoon, rushed a German sub-machine gun group who had taken buildings at an important street corner. With the infantry firing their sub-machine guns from the tanks, which were themselves blazing away, the three vehicles rushed the Germans and destroyed their position. The group then moved over to the other end of the factory district where another German attack was expected. Such small detachments, the best means of utilising armour in the unique conditions of street fighting, gave what support they could as another German offensive crashed on the Russian positions on October 14th. The Germans could not be stopped from taking the Tractor Plant and driving to the Volga in the north, cutting 62nd Army in two. Tanks now had to be repaired on the eastern banks of the Volga.

As the German infantry, with tank support, turned south on the 16th they ran across the T-34s of 84th Tank Brigade under the personal direction of Army Armoured Forces commander, Colonel Vainrub. The Soviet mediums, dug in under mounds of rubble, cut loose with their 76.2mm guns on the advancing PzKpfw III coming down Tramvaynaya Street at a range of about 100 metres. Soon over ten German tanks were ablaze and Soviet artillery and rocket fire was adding to the German discomfiture. The Germans could not see the well hidden Soviet tanks which dismissed more German vehicles as they tried to advance again. Only a heavy attack by Stukas and fighter bombers succeeded in indiscriminately blasting a path forward.

By late October the depth of the Russian defensive perimeter shrank to about 800-900 metres and the margin of survival became very slim indeed. Three knocked out Russian tanks were repaired and put together with thirty infantrymen recovered from their wounds and twelve men from H.Q. units to mount a counter attack covering the deployment of the desperately needed 45th Rifle Division. The Germans were also becoming exhausted and, despite its weakness, this counter attack led to much worried radio traffic about Soviet armour in action. By the end of October it was clear that German 6th Army had temporarily exhausted itself, but on November 11th it made one last try to take the city. More of the Volga bank fell into German hands. 62nd Army was now down to 19 tanks still fighting among its 47,000 men, carved by now into three isolated groups. Chuikov was at his 'last gasp' – but the tide was about to turn.

So far 1942 had not lived up to expectations for the Soviet armoured forces. The Stalingrad sector had not been the only area of defeat. In late July 121 tanks supporting Southern and North Caucasus Fronts along the lower Don had not been able to do a great deal against List's Army Group A which crossed the river and drove south. By the 27th T-34s and T-70s well emplaced and camouflaged against air reconnaissance, were helping to guard the River Sal at Martynovka. Once the Russians had made their presence felt in an ambush the 23rd Panzer Division quickly reacted holding the attention of the Russians frontally while sending its tanks into the Soviet flanks in the early hours of the 28th. In confused combat at ranges at 20-30 metres the Russian tanks were steadily knocked out; twelve T-34s and six T-60s falling to one German tank company alone. Anti-tank 'sticky' grenades were extra hazards the Russians had to face as well as 50mm and 75mm armour piercing rounds. By the end of the battle 77 Soviet tanks were claimed destroyed. The Russians had been surprised and outfought in a classic manner. There was little in the way of armour now left to stop the Germans sweeping down into the Caucasus. More tanks were brought in by rail, not only from the U.S.S.R. but also from Persia and the Anglo-American supply routes. British Tetrarchs added their limited strength to the Soviet defences. By November the Germans had been brought to a halt but only at the gates of Ordzhonikidze and Tuapse.

In the north, at the end of August, the Russians made yet another attempt to relieve Leningrad. The operation was planned to take the pressure off the south and pre-empt a German offensive known to be in the offing. To the south of Lake Ladoga on the 27th August, a rebuilt 2nd Shock Army thrust westwards towards Sinyavino and the River Mga; sixteen rifle divisions, nine rifle brigades, supported by five tank brigades with 300 tanks. These forces had been brought up in great secrecy, the tanks coming up to the front on heavily camouflaged railway wagons, and considerable surprise was achieved. A penetration of five miles was obtained but Manstein, just moved north to supervise the final German assault on Leningrad, was able to drive German infantry into the Soviet flanks and cut off most of 2nd Shock's infantry from the five leading tank brigades. The rest of the Russian forces tried to batter through to join up once more but by October 2nd, after merciless air and artillery bombardment of the 'pocket' it was finally liquidated and 244 Soviet tanks were captured or destroyed. The forces within Leningrad went over to the offensive also, but, despite attacks across the river which employed amphibious T-40s, little progress was possible against a strong German defence. Bridgeheads were obtained but the attack soon bogged down and in early October the Russians withdrew back across the river.

Things went a little better in the centre of the front where the Russians tried to pinch out the Rzhev salient in August. The Soviet tanks had some difficulties with the terrain as the poor roads and weak bridges were soon broken up and the tanks and motorised riflemen, already forced to operate strung out in long columns, got split up into small, weak groups. Attempts to use tank brigades as mobile 'penetration' units failed and as usual the armour reverted to the dispersed infantry support role. It was impossible to bring up supplies or artillery and there were still too few mobile engineers to get tanks and supply lorries moving through the difficult terrain. The very ability to detect good tank country seemed to be deficient. Still, even if the salient was not cut off, at least more German troops had to be brought in, diverted away from Stalingrad.

Slowly and expensively the Russians were learning new lessons. The Soviet tank troops were acquiring the experience that was the only counter to the reaction and neglect of the immediate pre-war years. Katukov's 'Professors' were being joined by an increasing number of crews and leaders who had survived disasters and drawn conclusions from them. They now knew to look for suitable lines of advance, properly reconnoitred; to attack along lines of least expectation, from flank and rear rather than frontally; to envelop rather than assault; to exploit accurate fire from the halt and from hull down positions; to keep their distance from the Germans to fully utilise the advantages of their still superior vehicles; above all, to concentrate their armour in decisive quantities and to back up their tanks with infantry, artillery, engineer and other support in formations with adequate training, flexibility and mobility for truly co-ordinated operations. Only thus would the Germans be defeated and

In a flurry of snow the T-34 'Rodina' (Motherland) roars into the centre of Stalingrad in January 1943.

6th Army, locked in combat in Stalingrad with long flanks on either side, held by ill equipped and motivated axis 'satellite' troops looked an inviting experiment in decisive battle.

Promising Victory

By November 1942 the Red Army had 15 tank and mechanised corps in front line service and 13 more in reserve. The new field service regulations, PU-42, set out their intended use; the tank corps were to be utilised in cooperation with the infantry to achieve a breakthrough, while mechanised corps would be reserved for exploitation thrusting deep behind enemy lines. The tank corps, therefore, was seen more as a source of extra NPP tanks than as a mobile force in their own right – although in the short term with the shortage of mechanised corps it had to double as a mobile force also. But it was still acceptable doctrine to divert even a mechanised corps' tank units to the initial breakthrough role – even though this would deplete its strength and lead to problems of reorganisation under difficult battle conditions when the time came for exploitation.

The tactics of all arms cooperation, however, were belatedly being perfected. 'Tank descents' of infantry were now confirmed as a vital part of armoured operations. In the assault, if opposition was not too serious, the infantrymen riding on the tanks scattered fire in all directions from their sub-machine guns to keep down the heads of the defenders and protect the tanks from stalkers. If anti-tank guns or other enemy strongpoints were encountered the 'descent' then jumped off to take troublesome positions in flank, to deal with the enemy forces using small arms, grenades and mortars. This was part of a whole new doctrine of coordinated warfare. A new directive NKO-325 of 16th October, 1942 exhorted the en masse use of tank formations and units at all levels with the closest cooperation of all arms under united command. As far as breakthrough NPP operations were concerned the following was prescribed – "artillery and infantry will be allotted the task of destroying enemy tanks, the reconnaissance and clearing of minefields, the aiding of tanks in overcoming various forms of natural and artificial tank obstacles, forming 'tank descents' and rapidly consolidating the captured objective or position. The main task of artillery is to provide continuous fire support to NPP tanks – particularly in destroying enemy tanks and anti-tank artillery in their wake. The primary task of aviation is to destroy enemy tanks and artillery and to cover the tactical approach of its own tanks by strikes from enemy aircraft". Once the breach had been made balanced and coordinated mobile forces could pour in to achieve a decisive success.

Such then were the doctrines in the minds of Soviet armoured commanders like Zhukov and Vasilevskii planning a decisive counter offensive at Stalingrad. On September 13th Stalin was presented with a plan, a major double envelopment offensive against the weakly held German flanks on either side of the city. At the end of September it was decided to revise the Soviet command structure in the Stalingrad area. Yeremenko's South Western Front now logically became Stalingrad Front and the old Stalingrad Front was split into Don and South West Fronts under Lieutenant Generals Rokossovskii and Vatutin. By the end of September Stalingrad and Don Fronts had the armoured strength of their eight armies built up to two tank corps and 18 tank brigades; 525 tanks in all about evenly divided between the two. The General Staff decided that twice this number of vehicles would have to be committed if a decisive victory was to be achieved.

Two tank armies, 3rd and 5th, were brought into 'special reserve' for the new offensive and the latter was moved to reinforce South West Front. XVII and XVIII Tank Corps were brought down from Voronezh Front at the beginning of October, to refit behind Don Front whose own IV Tank Corps was also pulled back to prepare for the offensive. Tank formations of all shapes and sizes, corps, brigades, regiments and battalions moved up for the grand offensive. South West Front's reinforcements included I and XXVI Tank Corps, 13th Tank Brigade and three tank regiments. Stalingrad Front was furnished with XIII Tank Corps and three tank brigades, one the 235th Flame-Thrower Tank Brigade.

Yeremenko also received one of the first mechanised corps, IV, a rather hastily assembled formation from a mixed bag of available units. IV Mechanised contained the survivors of XXVIII Tank Corps, as well as the remains of two well used tank brigades, 55th and 108th. Recently wounded personnel were rushed back to the front to provide experienced crews. By the middle of October IV Mechanised's experienced commander, Major General Volskii, had his requisite three mechanised brigades under command, 36th, 59th and 60th, each with a large tank regiment to support the lorried infantry. No less than three armoured car battalions were provided, although artillery support appears to have been limited to a Katyusha 'Guards Mortar Battalion'. Nevertheless 4th Mechanised was a powerful enough formation with its 220 tanks, 100 armoured cars, 2,000 trucks and 20,000 men.

In late October planning for Operation Uran (Uranus) was complete. Stalingrad Front was to smash north westwards to meet South Western Front striking down through the Don Bend. The two Fronts would meet in the Kalach-Sovietskii area cutting off the German forces in Stalingrad which would then be destroyed. Due to the longer distance some of their forces had to cover, over 110 kilometres, South West and Don Fronts would begin the offensive on November 9th. Stalingrad Front, with a maximum of only 80 kilometres to cover, would attack on the 10th. This was an operation well fitted to the short range shock power the Red Army had now built up. Advances of just over 100 kilometres were well within the capabilities of the existing Soviet armoured formations, whose tanks were being moved up to the front in the greatest secrecy, moving only by night and staying concealed by day.

By early November South West Front deployed three front line armies; from right to left 1st Guards, 5th Tank and 21st. 5th Tank Army was a very powerful force with about 350 tanks, I and XXVI Tank Corps, 8th Tank Brigade and an independent tank battalion to give the cutting edge for a cavalry corps, six rifle divisions and a motor cycle regiment. Twenty artillery regiments provided fire support and 1st Mixed Aviation Division provided organic on-call air cover directly subordinated to Army command. This mobile and flexible force was commanded by Romanenko, now a Lieutenant General. It was he who had taken such a strong line back in December, 1940 in favour of armoured 'shock armies'. Now he would have a chance to see what he could make of one. He was to mount the main attack out of the bridgehead held over the Don at Serafimovich. Chistyakov's 21st Army would attack on his left with the 150 tanks of IV Tank Corps, III Guards Cavalry Corps and six rifle divisions. After the two major breakthroughs on the first day the three tank corps and the cavalry units, reorganised in 'exploitation echelons', were to be pushed forward as hard as possible as the slower moving rifle formations encircled the Rumanians who held this sector of the Front. The tank corps would cross the Don and meet up with Stalingrad Front. Lorried infantry would follow up the tanks to consolidate the ground won.

Don Front, on Vatutin's left, was to attack from the Don bridgeheads east of Kletskaya with 65th Army under Lieutenant General Batov. This was the old 4th Tank Army but it had lost almost all its tanks in the previous fighting. On being taken over by Batov his Chief of Staff informed him it was '4 Tank Army' in truth – all guarding headquarters! Now he had two under strength tank brigades, 91st and 121st, with 24 tanks between them to support the attacks of his rifle divisions south eastwards to meet Galinin's 21st Army attacking south of Kachalinskaya. This would, hopefully, encircle the German armies caught west of the Don. Two more tank companies, about 14 vehicles, provided a belated reinforcement. Galinin had least had a tank corps, XVI, to exploit his breakthrough and he shared five tank brigades with 66th Army, whose infantry were to fight defensively on Don Front's left to tie down maximum German forces.

On the southern wing of the offensive Shumilov's 57th Army would concentrate two tank brigades and two rifle divisions on an eight mile front to punch a hole in the Axis lines in order that XIII Tank Corps, which had given up one of its tank regiments to support the breakthrough fighting, could be on its way by the end of the first day. To the south Trufanov's 51st Army, although diverting two of IV Mechanised's tank regiments to the NPP role in the opening fighting, also hoped to have its mobile exploitation echelons committed equally soon in order to 'demoralise the enemy rear' and meet South Western Front.

On November 9th orders were received postponing the offensive for a week as not all the forces earmarked were yet in position and there were still gross shortages of ammunition and supplies of all kinds. XIII Tank Corps lacked lorries for its motor rifle brigade and only a third of IV Mechanised's Infantry had trucks due to the fact that 150 such vehicles had been diverted to moving supplies and never returned. Logistics were a real problem with only limited rail capacity and a severe lack of motorised transport. Roads made muddy by the Autumn mud slowed down

Two T-34s approach a German strongpoint in the snow covered ruins of Stalingrad. The tank riders have dismounted and are ready to rush in with their grenades and sub machine-guns.

what trucks there were and the freezing of the Volga prevented pontoon bridges being used for bringing tanks over the river to Stalingrad Front. Barges had to be used instead and their capacity was limited due to particularly difficult river conditions. It was a considerable achievement in the circumstances to ferry 420 tanks across the river to Stalingrad Front in under three weeks. Except in the last urgent days all movement was made at night due to the danger of the Luftwaffe. I Tank Corps suffered some casualties due to air attack when it was caught in daylight crossing pontoon bridges over the Don to its forward positions with 5th Tank Army.

More time, however, meant that at least the tank crews and armoured commanders could go over the detailed plans for their attack once again. Planning was the Soviet Army's answer to the flexible initiative of the German Panzers. Final reconnaissances mapped out the enemy dispositions and Soviet troops were fully briefed on the lay-out of the German defences and how to deal with them, even down to which embrasures to shoot up with tank guns and into which trenches to throw hand grenades and Molotov cocktail petrol bombs. The concept even extended to mobile operations; before being brought to the front XXVI Tank Corps had exercised in just the sort of terrain to be expected in the Don Bend. They knew how to negotiate its dangerous ravines and gullies and the way to their objectives. German anti-tank obstacles were simulated. In the final days before the attack war games were held at all command levels to familiarise officers with what was required. As long as the plan worked out they would be fully in command of the situation. Volskii made sure that all IV Mechanised's men had the maximum benefit of local knowledge and inhabitants were interrogated on every detail of the terrain and recruited to guide the tanks. Techniques of 'all arms' cooperation were also worked out in detail. Tanks had two or three engineers attached to them to help them get over obstacles. Radios were now more easily available and special radio codes were devised to call in air support. It was a new model Soviet Army that prepared to go into action with 894 tanks and over a million men.

At 07.30 on Thursday, November 19th, the preliminary bombardment began on South Western and Don Fronts in misty conditions that precluded the use of aircraft. After almost 90 minutes heavy shelling the mixed 'NPP groups' of tanks and infantry moved forward. In the first wave came heavy, radio equipped KVs, accompanied by infantry on foot to search out and engage the more difficult strongpoints, especially anti-tank positions. Five hundred yards behind were the T-34s with their 'descents', about ten infantrymen riding on board each tank, who dismounted to deal with bunkers and other identified enemy strongpoints. As they leapt down, the tanks kept going shooting at the embrasures, while the infantry opened up with small arms and hurled grenades. Artillery fire was closely controlled by radio, with a barrage creeping in front of the tanks as well as direct fire to crack open particularly difficult strongpoints. Each tank battalion was allocated an artillery battery for such close support. Some tanks towed field guns forward so that they could reach targets deeper into the enemy positions. As the opposition cracked and breaches appeared in the enemy lines a third wave of tanks and infantry composed like the second but also containing lighter T-70s pressed on ahead finding paths into the enemy rear. The 3rd Rumanian Army resisted bravely at first despite a lack of proper anti-tank equipment, and Soviet air strikes as the weather cleared. By noon the Soviet 5th Tank Army had advanced less than two miles. Parts of the Army's tank corps had been committed to the initial fighting (XXVI Tank Corps' 216th Tank Brigade was put under the command of 24th Rifle Division) but at 12.30 the decision was taken to commit the rest of both corps en masse to achieve a decisive penetration. The two remaining tank brigades, 19th and 173rd, spearheaded XXVI's drive, moving forward in four columns. On their right I Tank Corps now under Major General V.V. Butkov's command, widened the breakthrough to 13 kilometres. The fog and snow made navigation difficult and the T-70s had some difficulty finding a way through the difficult going. Rumanian morale collapsed as Soviet tanks reached the rear areas of the Axis position. Their defences began to fall apart and the troops streamed back in disorganised retreat. The infantry of 47th Guards Rifle Division riding on the supporting tanks of 8th Guards Tank Brigade followed in pursuit. By evening the Russians had advanced 20 kilometres by-passing the tanks and anti-tank guns of the depleted German 22nd Panzer Division and easily dealing with the PzKpfw 38(t) of the Rumanian armoured division, which crashed unwittingly into the advancing Russian armour.

To the left 21st Army had released its mobile forces even earlier, at mid-day, to overcome Rumanian opposition; IV Tank Corps and III Cavalry Corps operating in mixed groups had advanced over 32 kilometres by the end of the day. As XXVI Tank Corps also pressed on through the night, using compasses and local guides for navigation, headlights were switched on to make the going easier. The headquarters town of Perelazovskii was captured at dawn.

Now Stalingrad Front prepared to set the other jaw of the pincers in motion. Again the weather was foggy which delayed the opening of the barrage, but at 09.30 Yeremenko ordered the assault to begin. After 45 minutes 422nd Rifle Division, supported by XIII Tank Corps' 176th Tank Brigade, went over to the attack along with the rest of 57th Army in the usual tank/infantry 'NPP groups'. To the south 51st Army attacked at the original time, 07.30, with 55th and 158th Infantry Brigades advancing on a three mile front, supported by 4th Mechanised's 55th and 158th Tank Regiments. Five T-34s fell to the guns of 6th Rumanian Corps but the bewildered 'satellite' troops soon began to surrender.

XIII Tank Corps began its main advance in two columns at 14.00 but was slowed down by its 'marching' infantry. The Russians were forced to bring their infantry into battle by train on the Kotelnikovo railway line! Now the XIII ran into the German tanks, infantry and artillery of 29th Motorised Division which was rushed up to shore up the Axis' lines. As the mist lifted a battle of encounter developed in which the Germans were able to exploit their continued superiority in fast reactions and initiative. As the first T-34s succumbed to long 75mm guns of the PzKpfw IV the Russians were thrown into confusion. More tanks fell to the 50mm guns of PzKpfw III and the German artillery soon demolished the Russian troop trains. The Soviet attack was halted.

To the south there were also problems. Volskii of IV Mechanised had developed 'cold feet' at the last minute and tried to approach Stalin to get the Whole 'Uran' operation called off on the grounds of insufficient forces being available. He was unsuccessful, but his attitude perhaps partly accounts for the dilatoriness of his Corps' actions. It is easy to criticise Volskii for this although later in the war he was to prove himself an armoured leader of considerable daring. Facing the well handled German Panzers he was right to be careful about his flanks and demand overwhelming superiority of strength. Whatever the matter the start order was given at 11.30 but only at 13.00 were the three mechanised brigades set in motion. It took time to redeploy the two tank regiments back to their mobile role. IV Mechanised's crews do not seem to have been as well briefed and prepared as their counterparts in the northern tank corps. The 60th Mechanised Brigade, tasked to advance along a road, lost its way in the snow. The other two brigades got caught up in minefields and instead of advancing in the columns as ordered tried to find security in advancing along the same road as the 60th which was soon an impassable bog, jammed with supply trucks. By nightfall Volskii had lost 50 tanks and the first objective, Verkhne - Tsaritsynsk had still not been reached. The fate of XIII Tank Corps to the north threatened Volskii's right flank. If the 29th Motorised crashed into his confused formations the result might be disaster. His left flank also seemed exposed and although a gap of more than 20 miles wide now yawned in the right flank of VI Rumanian Corps the Mechanised Corps was only at Abganerovo by dawn on the 21st.

IV Mechanised finally halted at Zety to replenish with fuel and ammunition. Yeremenko was becoming hourly more frustrated with Volskii's performance and early on the 22nd issued direct and strong instructions to advance. The Corps did so, slowly, 36th Mechanised Brigade being sent ahead to Sovietskii with 26th Tank Regiment providing the armoured battering ram. Carrying 'not only the honour of the Brigade but of the whole Corps' the tanks and motorised infantry were in Sovietskii on time at mid-day on the 22nd.

XXVI Tank Corps under its more 'press on' commander, Major General A. G. Rodin, captured Perelazovskii on the 20th, re-fuelled with German oil, and, having advanced 40 kilometres spent the night at Ostrov. A reconnaissance force was sent on towards the Don, which reported the main German defence zone to be 20 kilometres distant. It was however learned from a local peasant woman that the Kalach bridge was still intact and the defenders were in ignorance of the proximity of the Russian forces. Rodin now decided to form a special infiltration group of five tanks from 157th Tank Brigade and motorised infantry put into German lorries, under Colonel Filippov. This unit was tasked with taking the vital bridge and set out at 05.00 on the 21st to move down to the bridge in German marching formation. The tanks drove through the unsuspecting German lines with lights on. The area was used for anti-tank training and Soviet tanks were a common sight. They were, therefore, able to drive right on to the bridge and the infantry quickly dealt with the sentries. Filippov organised an all round defence as the rest of the Brigade fought its way through the German defensive positions to the north. In mid-afternoon the advance Soviet main forces, under Major Filipenko, joined up with Filippov's group and held the vital crossing until the rest of XXIII Tank Corps moved up. Shortly after 10.00 on the 22nd the Corps took Kalach itself.

By the 23rd Kravchenko's IV Tank Corps was also over the river and its 45th Tank Brigade joined up during the afternoon with 36th Mechanised Brigade in the designated area east of Sovietskii. The Soviet plan had succeeded. The whole of German 6th Army and part of 4th Panzer Army were cut off, over 280,000 men, 100 tanks, 2,000 guns and 10,000 trucks.

The Russians estimated that they had only caught some 90,000 Germans in their trap but when they struck eastwards at the 'pocket' on November 24th they soon found that the enemy was in much greater strength. The attacks by XXVI and IV Tank Corps, now allocated to 21st Army, and the other forces surrounding the Germans made some progress, but the Germans were able to halt the Russian advances. By early December Don and Stalingrad Fronts had 340 tanks surrounding the besieged 6th Army but this was deemed insufficient to complete its destruction. Another Army, 2nd Guards combining two infantry Corps (both 'Guards') and II Guards Mechanised Corps moved down to reinforce Don Front. In order to defend the western wall of the encirclement from the expected German counter attacks another elite formation, 5th Shock Army with General P.A. Rotmistrov's VII Tank Corps was subordinated to Stalingrad Front and slotted into place between 5th Tank and 51st Armies. The Russians expected the German counter attack to take place on the shortest approach between the German lines and Stalingrad, in other words north east of Nizhne Chirskaya.

On the 12th the expected offensive began but the new German Army Group Don commander, Manstein, chose the indirect approach, where the distance was greatest but the Soviet forces weakest. Sixth and 23rd Panzer Divisions made some progress north east of Kotelnikovo against the infantry and cavalry of Trufanov's 51st Army supported by a single outnumbered tank brigade; 77 tanks against almost 250. Now, however, XIII Tank Corps, as well as the 235th Tank Brigade with its flame throwing T-34s and elements of IV Mechanised were quickly committed and a major tank battle raged for three days. The Germans still rated the Russians as inferior in terms of training and coordination but they themselves were running into supply difficulties due to the wintry conditions. The Russians were somewhat under strength due to the losses of the previous fighting – by December 15th IV Mechanised was down to only 70 tanks – and there were probably not many more Soviet tanks than German in action. To the Germans though it seemed as if they were outnumbered almost two to one as the concentrated groups of T-34s pressed into the attack. Russian tank crews were now good enough to stop the German advance and convince the panzer crews of the continued inferiority of even their new long-gunned PzKpfw III compared with the T-34. In the close fighting the Soviets were able to use their 76.2mm guns to good effect to open up even the latest up-armoured German tanks. IV Mechanised drove 6th Panzer out of Verkhne Kumsky on the 15th and the town repeatedly changed hands. The corps renamed III Guards Mechanised Corps was eventually driven back on the River Myshkova. It was now subordinated to Malinovskii's 2nd Guards Army, whose troops were thrown into action as they arrived along the river line, shortages of fuel causing many tanks to be used as static pillboxes. Nevertheless the Germans were becoming exhausted and although they gained a few bridgeheads they could advance no further.

Roughly camouflaged with whitewash, and with their callsigns painted on the turret, two T-34s advance over snow coverd country. The tanks appear to have a mixture of steel and rubber treaded wheels, but the gun overhang suggests that they are T-34/76Cs.

By now a new major Soviet offensive had opened. At the beginning of December Operation 'Saturn' had been approved, an attack by Voronezh and South West Fronts aimed at Millerovo and Rostov, cutting right across the rear of the German front in the south. A powerful attack would also be made due eastwards. The German counter attack at Stalingrad meant that the operation had to be postponed and it was eventually scaled down into a 'Little Saturn' attack over the Don into the left flank of Manstein's Army Group aimed at the airfields that were keeping 6th Army supplied in Stalingrad itself. On the 16th three Soviet armies, 3rd, 1st Guards and 67th went over to the attack deploying four tank and one mechanised corps (I Guards) with strong air support. 8th Italian Army holding this sector was overwhelmed. Badonov's XXIV Tank Corps advanced 240 kilometres in five days, a true 'blitzkrieg' rate of advance and attacked the supply airfield at Tatsinskaya on Christmas Eve. The sleepy Germans were taken completely by surprise and the T-34s caused chaos in the fog, destroying several aircraft. The Germans reacted swiftly; 6th Panzer Division moved up to reinforce the local 11th Panzer Division which had been covering the left flank of the Stalingrad relief. The German armour surrounded the Russians around Tatsinkaya and trapped the Soviet tank corps. Attempts to relieve it failed and it was destroyed in night combat, although some survivors did manage to fight their way to the Soviet lines.

Perhaps Volskii had been right; against the quick reacting mobile German Panzertruppen one operated with open flanks at one's peril. On the 31st, the tanks of XXV Tank Corps on XXIV's left were running confidently forward with headlights on towards the ford at Maryevka over the Bystraya stream. 6th Panzer deployed its powerful 75mm anti-tank guns to hold them frontally while the German armour pressed in from flank and rear. A fierce night battle developed at close range with the Russians thrown into considerable confusion. Both sides tried ramming but the odds were finally with the experienced Germans: by morning 90 T-34s littered the battlefield.

On Christmas Eve 2nd Guards and 51st Armies had gone over to the offensive. VII Tank Corps transferred over to replace the exhausted III Guards Mechanised Corps moved with I Guards Rifle Corps through Verkhne Kumsky. VI Mechanised Corps, brought out of Stavka reserve to reinforce 2nd Guards Army, smashed, together with II Guards Mechanised, into the right flank of LVII Panzer Corps towards Ketelnikovo. On the 27th a freshly refitted III Guards Mechanised Corps, together with XIII Tank Corps, struck even further to the left against 4th Rumanian Army. By this time the Germans were fighting for Ketelnikovo as VII Tank swung round from the north west and there were masses of KVs, T-70s and T-34s pushing into the enemy rear. A double envelopment forced Army Group Don, a disaster that would cause not only its own loss but the cutting off of Army Group A in the Caucasus. On the 28th Hitler reluctantly authorised the German forces to move back to a line 240 kilometres west of Stalingrad.

On the 10th January seven Soviet Armies of Rokossovskii's Don Front attacked the encircled Germans in Stalingrad in Operation 'Ring'. T-34s and infantry swept into the German positions and, despite losses to German anti-tank and anti-aircraft guns, made several penetrations. After two weeks heavy fighting Chuikov's 62nd Army joined up with Chistyakov's 21st. By February 2nd the last Germans surrendered, 91,000 prisoners were in Soviet hands and over 200,000 German soldiers had been lost. The Russians had won their first great victory of the war.

Already they were after a greater prize, the entire southern set of German armies. On January 12th a massive armour and infantry attack began further up the Don, aimed at Kharkov and the Donets basin. Voronezh Front mounted its assault with two tank corps and eight tank brigades to give armoured weight to its four armies. Two of these 40th and 3rd Tank were to strike on the right and left respectively in a classic short range armoured envelopment meeting 80 kilometres behind the Axis lines and trapping 2nd Hungarian Army in between. Originally the assault was planned for the 14th but a preliminary reconnaissance attack on the 12th caused such chaos that the assault was immediately pushed in. The Russians used T-34s fitted with mine rollers to clear a path through the Axis minefields. This was the first time such tactics had been used – normally Soviet tanks 'swept' minefields by the direct means of driving across them! There was close artillery cooperation with the assaulting NPP groups to deal with troublesome strongpoints. The Soviet tanks had few difficulties with counter attacks by the mixed bag of tanks of the Hungarian Armoured Division and by the 18th the encirclement had been consummated with few losses; 86,000 prisoners fell into Soviet hands as 40th Army moved into the flank of German 2nd Army, forcing the evacuation of Voronezh.

Further south where the Don flows to Rostov the Russians were reacting slowly to the German withdrawal. Yeremenko's South Front was below establishment, it was 320 kilometres from its railhead, the Germans were resisting firmly and the arrival of the warmer weather made the going almost impossible. Nevertheless on the 20th January 2nd Guards Army sent Rotmistrov's III Guards Tank Corps (the erstwhile VII Tank) over the Manych at Manychskaya, thrusting towards Bataysk. A leading detachment was assembled under Colonel Yegorov with 8 T-34s, 3 T-70s, 9 half-tracks, 5 armoured cars and 200 accompanying infantrymen. II Guards Mechanised was sent down to cross the Manych at Spornyy, while III Guards Mechanised was leading 51st Army further south still coming up on Bataysk from the south east. Rotmistrov's Corps would attack Bataysk on the 23rd, but now the German 16th Motorised Division interposed itself across the supply lines of II Guards Mechanised at Spornyy. An advanced force got as far as Samodurovka on the lines of communication of III Guards Tank. The main body of the Corps was now tied down in futile attempts to reduce these German positions and its advance guard, received the full force of the 11th Panzer Division to the west. With five T-34s and two T-70s knocked out Yegorov was forced to break back eastwards. The Russians now had to fight for their bridgehead as 11th Panzer and 16th Motorised threw themselves against it. T-34s dug in 'a la Stalingrad' provided a formidable anti-tank defence but the Soviets were eventually outmanoeuvred. The Germans took Manychskaya and 20 wrecked T-34s: 2nd Guards Army had shot its bolt. The heavy fighting of the previous weeks had virtually destroyed its armoured strength; on the 26th January III Guards Tank Corps had only 14 tanks left, II Guards Mechanised 8 and V Guards Mechanised (the erstwhile VI Mechanised) 7. As Rotmistrov reported: " In view of their situation and their heavy losses the troops are no longer engaged in any active operations at the moment". On January 27th Hitler finally gave instructions to Army Group A to withdraw: there was still a corridor through which they could do so.

At the beginning of February the Russians moved forward in a new surge. Voronezh Front began Operation 'Star' aimed at the capture of Kharkov while Vatutin's South West Front struck down towards the Sea of Azov. Although the Germans were able to keep the Russian tanks at bay with anti-tank guns and '88s' while 1st Panzer Army completed its withdrawal through Rostov, the city finally fell to a mixed group of tanks and cavalry of 44th Army (North Caucasus Front) on the 6th. Southern Front, now commanded by Malinovskii, pushed the Germans back north of the city. Another major double envelopment threatened the southern wing of the Ostfrot. The Germans pulled back to the line of the River Mius, where an attack by IV Guards Mechanised Corps was taken in flank and defeated but South Western Front's Army striking towards the Dniepr posed the major threat. On the 11th Stalin, convinced the Germans were collapsing, ordered South West Front to 'cut off the German southern group'. The forces to achieve this feat comprised firstly Major General Kharitonov's 6th Army with two tank corps, a cavalry corps and two rifle corps which would cross the Dniepr between Dnepropetrovsk and Zaporozhe. On the left was a special operational group, 'Tank Group Popov', a powerful army size formation with four tank corps, two tank brigades, three rifle divisions and a ski brigade. Lieutenant General M. M. Popov, recently transferred from 5th Shock Army, was to strike with this powerful force west of Slavyansk towards Stalino and Mariupol.

The Soviet forces had been considerably weakened after their advance of about 650 kilometres and Popov, although powerful on paper, only had a spearhead of 145 operational tanks and 13,000 men to carry out his advance. Krasnoarmeyskoye fell but the Russians soon outran supplies and again the danger of operating with exposed flanks against skilled armoured troops became all too apparent. As the S.S. Division 'Wiking' held the Russians in front, 11th Panzer Division sliced across the armoured group's supply lines. On the 18th the hapless Popov reported "all wheels are standing still". As another Panzer Division, 7th, joined in the destruction, Popov's immobilised tanks and infantry were cut up into individual brigades and battalions by the German tanks and motorised infantry and smashed in detail. On the 23rd Popov desperately radioed to Vatutin asking for help and informing the Army Commander of his lack of everything from tanks to artillery, ammunition and food. These calls fell on deaf ears until the evening of the 24th when the magnitude of the disaster finally dawned on the Front Command and offensive operations were halted. More armour desperately tried to stop the counter attacking Germans reaching the Donets, but by the 28th they were on the river and 250 Soviet tanks littered the battlefield behind them.

Although 6th Army's offensive had begun well it eventually fared no better. With 150 T-34s and KVs of XXV Tank Corps racing through scattered resistance it got as far as Pavlograd, which fell on the 18th. The next day XXV Tank Corps advanced still further to Stelnikovo across one of the major supply lines to the Mius positions and a mere 65 kilometres from Zaporozhye, where Hitler himself was meeting Manstein. Now, however, as the Russians began to run short of serviceable tanks the German counter attack began. A German infantry division counter attacked at Senelnikovo and its 75mm self-propelled tank destroyers held off the T-34s. Then on the 19th the S.S. Division 'Das Reich' with heavy air support slammed into 6th Army's right flank with 6th and 7th Panzer Divisions driving in on the left. XXV Tank Corps was soon cut off and on the 24th, with Popov's Group also in deep trouble, Vatutin called off all offensive operations. The 3rd Tank Army to the north was ordered to come to the rescue but the Luftwaffe disrupted its assembly. Again the Russians were pushed back to the Donets with even greater losses, some 364 tanks.

The Russian attempt at a truly decisive victory had failed. No less than 25 tank brigades had been destroyed. 69th Army, trying to hold the line east of Kharkov, had no operational tanks left, neither had 64th Army, rushed over from Operation Ring. Belgorod fell but now the mud came to Russia's rescue once more. The German offensive bogged down, leaving the Russians still in possession of a wide salient around Kursk. By the time the Germans struck against this once more the Red Army would be a little better prepared.